Surviving the wait. How I learned to be still and wait on God

Published by: Deetra La'Rue Benn

This book or parts thereof may not be reproduced in any form, stored in a retrieval system, or transmitted in any form by any means—electronic, mechanical, photocopy, recording, or otherwise—without prior written permission of the publisher, except as provided by United States of America copyright law.

Scripture quotations marked NLT are from the Holy Bible, New Living Translation Version, copyright © 1996, 2004, 2007, 2015. Used by permission of Tyndale House Publishers. All rights reserved.

Copyright © 2021 by Deetra La'Rue Benn

All rights reserved

Visit the Author's website at www.notesbylarue.com

Dedication

First, I'd like to thank my mother, Thelma R. Cargill, for your constant support, both emotionally and financially. Thank you for every phone call to check on me, your constant prayers, and for being there in my times of need. This book is dedicated to those who feel God is not moving fast enough, taking too long, or simply doing nothing at all. There are times in your life you will become tired, weary, and beyond impatient with waiting, but He does promise to give you rest. It is so easy to take matters into your own hands, because you feel you can handle your situation better and quicker than He can. However, do not try to expedite things on your own. It is when we try to do things our way, that we cause ourselves to get out of alignment with God's purpose and will for our lives. Whether you're about to enter a storm, in the midst of one, or are on your way out, I have a word for you. There is a time for everything to take place in our lives, and when the time is right, God will make it happen. No matter what you're up against, God is with you as you are facing it, even when it feels He's not near. I hope you enjoy the hidden gems, more than anything, I hope you be still and wait for God to move in your life.

Table of Contents

Angry with God……………………………………………………………………..1

The Layover……………………………………………………………………….3

When everyone is moving, but you………………………………………………..6

Pick up your bat…………………………………………………………………..10

More than petals and feathers …………………………………………………...11

If only you would have listened…………………………………………………..15

Relieved…………………………………………………………………………..17

Giant Faith……………………………………………………………………….20

Every step counts………………………………………………………………...21

A different agenda……………………………………………………………….25

Now is not the time………………………………………………………………27

Wait on the promise……………………………………………………………...30

Change of plans………………………………………………………………….32

Driven in a different direction…………………………………………………...40

Traveling through impossible circumstances……………………………………43

Can't hardly wait………………………………………………………………...44

Detours…………………………………………………………………………..45

Transportation problems…………………………………………………………47

Hold on, it'll get better…………………………………………………………...48

Hurting to heal…………………………………………………………………...52

A purpose for the flames………………………………………………………...56

Looking for the rain……………………………………………………………...59

Buried (You've been planted) Pt. I………………………………………………61

Not yet (You've been planted) Pt. II……………………………………………..62

The emergence (You've been planted) Pt. III……………………………………64

Just ripe (You've been planted) The conclusion…………………………………65

Surviving the wait………………………………………………………………..75

Angry with God

Am I the only one who gets angry with God? I can't think of a time when I wasn't, but if I had to take a guess, I'd say it was during the highlights of my life. I'm pretty sure that most people would say the same. If we're honest with ourselves, when things are going fine for us, we're just as happy as we can be. However, the minute things start to go downhill, we blame God, and ask an endless amount of questions. "God, why did you let me lose my job?" "Why did you allow my mom to die?" "Why did you let my child get sick?" "Why did you not stop any of it, when you are capable of doing anything?" I've been very vocal about my misfortunes and struggles with poverty. I couldn't understand why God would allow me to endure the horrific conditions I did, especially if He loves me.

Why would He permit all those bad things that happened to me, when He could've simply stopped it? I'm sure you can imagine that I was one angry kid. Besides, I didn't ask to be here, yet I had to suffer because I was. In fact, I didn't ask for a lot of things, but one thing I did ask, and that was for God to deliver me from my pain. I thought, if you aren't willing to change my situation, then at least change the way it makes me feel. Needless to say, the only thing that changed, was how I felt about God. I went from loving to pray, to declaring it'd do no good, considering the fact that all of my prayers went unanswered (although I'd later learn they hadn't). For most of us, later seems to be the problem. We feel we shouldn't have to wait for anything, but if we didn't, we wouldn't have the need for God.

Just think, if He answered every prayer request the minute we made them, we wouldn't know what it means to wait, let alone the importance of it. I get it! Nobody wants to wait, at least I know I don't. Yet, when we find ourselves waiting, it could be for a number of reasons. The biggest, is that God is working things out for us, even if we can't see it. Sadly, I can't tell you how many times I thought that He was doing nothing (other than allowing me to suffer), but unbeknownst to me, He was up to something. He was shifting things around and working it all out for my good, but He needed time to do it, which is another one of our problems.

Clearly, we have a lot of problems, not to mention, a designated timeline for how and when things are to happen in our lives, but we there's one important thing to remember, that we often forget. God operates in Kairos time, and not our traditional clocking system, so He's not subjected to our deadlines. In other words, God is saying, you don't tell me what to do! Psalms 90:4 tells us, "A thousand years in your sight are like a day that has just gone by, or like a watch in the night" (NLT).

Yet and still, we'll ask God, "What took you so long to get here?" Only for Him to reply, "I'm not late, but right on time." Everything takes time, and it takes us realizing that God knows exactly what He's doing, so we might as well let Him do it. Griping and complaining won't help. Begging and pleading won't help, but what does help, is if we let go and trust God. It's so much easier said than done, but when it's all said and done, you'll understand why you had to wait. Of course we don't understand things now, but when we see why we had to wait, we'll thank God that we did. Besides, we have no clue what God has in store for us. Perhaps He's making us wait, so we won't be overwhelmed by our blessings. On the other hand, it could be that we're not ready. Whichever the case, be patient, be still, but most importantly, wait on God.

The Layover

I'm stuck, and I have been for quite some time now

As each day passes, I can't help but wonder if I'll ever board

Or will I continue to experience yet another delay?

Don't get me wrong, I don't mind waiting

Because I'm for certain it's for a very good reason

It has to be, after all, I've been waiting on it for years

However, I'd like to know what's so "special" that it's taking me years to get?

I'm exhausted, and at this point, I'm tired of sitting still

I'm ready to fly, no better yet, soar

But I can't, because for some reason God is keeping me grounded

Who knows, maybe He's protecting me from casualty

But it's not like I haven't flown before

So, I don't understand what the big deal is, or maybe I am the big deal

Because of my fragileness, God knows I've got to be handled with extreme care

Therefore, He won't just trust anything to carry His most precious cargo

But that still doesn't change the fact that I'm stuck!

What's crazy is that no matter how hard I've tried to take flight

My plans managed to get derailed, and I'm left wondering what did I do wrong?

Because in my eyes, I did all that I knew how right

Truth be told, I'm over this and I am ready to go!

God can You hear me? Are you even there?

You've had more than enough time to get this thing going

So, why am I still here? Are you afraid that I'll try to takeover

Just as I've done all the other times and crashed and burned?

Rather than have me make an unnecessary SOS, You jump right in and save me

In fact, You've always saved me, especially from what I thought was best for me

I'm so glad You thought more for me, than I did for myself

Had I done things my way, I would've never witnessed this journey

Let alone enjoyed it

As I reflect and look at things from Your perspective

I'm exactly where You want me to be

You've placed me in a position of preparation

Making sure everything is just right, and from the looks of it

My wait won't be much longer, and I'll be connecting soon

Until then, I'm going to sit still, be patient and enjoy ***the layover***

For thirteen years, I worked for a company I gave my all to. Although it had its ups and downs, I enjoyed what I did and being of service to others. Over the course of two years in that role, I realized the position I was in, was no longer one I wanted to hold. I tried relentlessly to take flight, but for reasons unknown, I was still employed there (you'll read more on this later). I had an immense feeling of suffocation, fright, and frantic thoughts of being stuck. I was petrified, because I tried so many times to get away, only to end up nowhere.

During that time, I wanted to fly to my next destination, but God wouldn't allow me. At that point, I realized I was in the middle of a layover. I was so disappointed, because I wanted out of that place! I didn't think it to be fair that I had to stay grounded, while everyone else was flying high. I wanted to know what it felt like to soar, but I couldn't seem to takeoff. I've tried to get on a different flight, but I wasn't permitted to board, because there wasn't a seat available for me. Exhausted but not giving up, I tried every other possible way to leave, but no matter what I did or which way I turned, I never did move. Although I know God knows what's best, it hurts when you see that everyone is moving, but you.

You may be in a similar position and are overwhelmed with feelings of being stuck, but I can assure you, you aren't. It's easy to become distracted by what everyone else is doing, that you miss out on what God is doing in your life. It's understandable that you want out of your situation, but suppose God is keeping you there, because He's still situating your next move. Of course, it's much easier said than done, but hang tight just a little bit longer, because God is preparing you for the flight you've always dreamed of. I hope you're ready, because once you takeoff, it's only up from there!

When everyone is moving, but you

One of my biggest pet peeves, is being stuck in traffic! Just the mere thought of waiting, let alone for hours, is enough to make my blood boil. As a struggling waiter (not to be confused with stewardess), sitting still drives me insane, because I know what needs to be done, yet I have no control over the situation. I have a million things to do and a thousand places to be, but since I can't regulate traffic, I can't go anywhere. Sadly, I have no choice but to sit in frustration, be patient and wait until the way is clear. Inch by inch, I feel myself progressing, but I'm just not moving fast enough. I look over to my right and see an opening, so I quickly try to jump in that lane. The car that sits behind me notices it too, and immediately pulls forward, leaving me right where I am, stuck!

However, I'm not really stuck; I'm just at a standstill waiting for God to move me. Although I'm extremely successful and thriving, I have an extreme sense of urgency to do "something." I don't care what it could possibly be, I must keep moving, because I can't afford to wait. Rather than stay in my lane and be still until it's time to move, I try to jump into someone's lane, because theirs is moving faster than mine. How many times can you say you've done this? We're so antsy to get to our next destination, that watching others move when you aren't, can be a bit of disappointment. It's not to say you aren't happy for them (in most cases, some people aren't), but you start to question, "When will it be my time?"

To answer your question, when God says it's time. Whatever He has for you, is reserved just for you! It does not matter if it takes you months or years to get there, it will still be there when you arrive. God is not on a timeline, you are. He's not in a rush, you are. He's not going to give you what you want, when you want it, but He will give it to you when you need it. Just because you see someone else is moving, doesn't mean that you aren't. You're just not moving the way you want to, because God knows what's best for you. What do you suppose would happen, if God immediately gave you exactly what you wanted, when you asked for it? Would you be happy? Overwhelmed? Stressed? Do you think you'd be grateful or regretful?

I know a lot of you are in situations you've grown beyond tired of. You want out so bad and will stop at nothing to be let loose. However, God is not going to release you, until it's time to move! For 13 years, I worked for a company I loved. There were so many days I didn't want to go to work, but I continued, because I had to provide for myself and the people I was hired to serve. After my first few years of being there, I was ready to move onto something else. I no longer loved my job or enjoyed what I did, and getting up for work every day, felt like a chore. This continued for the next 7 years, until God was ready for my next assignment. Ironically, the number 7 biblically represents completeness, so now I see why my time there was done.

As I stated earlier, God is not going to release you, until it's time for you to move. I regretted all the years I stayed in that position, but I would've regretted it more, had I left and not waited on God. I was there for a reason, and I had to go through what I did, in order to be able to handle what was to come later down the line. There were so many times I tried to run, but I was always met with a brick wall. I didn't care where I went as long as I was not there! During my many failed attempts to escape, God would always say, "Just wait on me." However, that was the issue, *waiting*. I'm an impatient person, not to mention, extremely anxious. I want everything to happen on my command, and when things don't, I take issue to it, but I always end up running back to God for help. The weight of it all becomes too much to handle, but I know there's nothing He can't do.

God can do anything but fail! I know it pains you to trust the process and wait on Him, but it's what's best. You can try to do as I did, and leave your job, but it doesn't matter how many job applications you complete or interviews you have, you're going to remain exactly where you are, until God says it's time. Until then, just enjoy the process. I know it can be hard to enjoy something that you're clearly over, or something that you're in, and desperately want out of. It's very difficult at times, when you're seeking God, and it seems He's not there. It can be quit challenging to continue to pray when everything's gone unanswered. It can be so draining to constantly cry out for help, and no one comes to your rescue. Keep in mind, "They that wait on the Lord. Shall renew their strength. They shall mount up on wings, just like an eagle and soar. They shall run and not be weary, they shall walk and never faint. They that wait" (Isaiah 40:31, NLT).

All you've got to do is just wait! It's so easy to say, yet incredibly hard to do, especially when you are tired of waiting. We're not operating on our time, but *Kairos* time, which means God will move at the proper time. It doesn't matter what you do to try and expedite the process, nothing will change until God changes it. There's nothing you can do or need to do to help Him, because He's "able to do everything exceedingly and abundantly more than you can ever hope for" (Ephesians 3:20, NLT). Whatever it is that you're waiting and praying to God for, keep on waiting and "Don't grow weary in doing good, for at the right time, you will reap the harvest" (Galatians 6:9, NLT).

Peddling nowhere

Have you ever seen someone struggling to ride a bike up a hill, only for them to continuously roll back down? No matter how many times they tried, it seemed as if they were peddling nowhere? Had you stuck around long enough, what do you supposed happened next? They finally made it to the top, or they quit after many failed attempts? If you went with the aforementioned, you're probably right. If you went with the latter, you're probably the cyclist. For most of your life, you've struggled. Whether you've struggled with poverty, loving yourself, finding the right job, your finances, finishing school, getting pregnant, quitting a bad habit, drinking, gambling, and the list goes on and on.

Most of us have struggled, and while some people have overcome, there are still others struggling to make it through. They've been peddling for years, and still haven't managed to make it anywhere. After seeing so many people happily pass them, especially the ones that were with them in the struggle, they begin to wonder if they'll ever get the chance to joy ride. In order to find out, they mustn't stop peddling. Don't quit because you think you haven't gotten anywhere. Take a look around you. I guarantee you aren't in the position you were in 5 years ago. You've made progressed, just not at the speed in which you were hoping.

It doesn't matter how great the struggle, what's important, is that you never stop peddling. Don't worry about those who've gone on ahead of you. Focus on climbing the hill that's ahead of you. Once you make it to the top, look down and help others to make the climb. It doesn't matter if you have to push them up, don't stop until they've reached the top. Remember, always help, when it's within your power to do so.

Pick up your bat

Kids are so cute and precious! I'm sure most people would agree. When my nieces and nephew played softball and baseball, I attended mostly all of their games, to show my support, and because I enjoyed the sport. I can remember many days passing the tee-ball playing field, but not before stopping to watch a play or two. I'd smile every time I saw a little batter come to the plate to take his/her swing. Although most times they'd miss, they never stopped swinging. Of course, laughter erupted, and shouts of "awe" echoed the stadium, but while most people thought it to be funny, I found it rather interesting.

I often questioned, "How is it that children between the ages of 4-7 saw an opportunity, took a swing at it, and wouldn't stop swinging until they hit their target. Yet so many adults see an opportunity, swing, strike out, then drop their bat and go back into the dugout, all because they didn't hit a homerun. Don't throw your opportunity to the ground, and walk away, because you didn't get it right on the first try. Pick up your bat! Like those children, so many of you are playing baseball. You want nothing more than to win, but you aren't doing what's necessary to get it. You've been at it forever, and nothing's change, so you feel it's best to quit the game.

Following in the children's footsteps, you have to be persistent and never give up. Things take time, and I know you think God is slowly taking His. Stop rushing to hit, and focus on getting your form right, so you'll be in position to receive what God is about to throw your way. When He pitches, you better be ready to swing. It may take you awhile to find your groove and rhythm, but it's okay, because God won't move until you are ready. The question is, "Are you?"

More than petals and feathers

There are so many people who don't like to wait, particularly, on God. After years of praying and not getting an answer, you can't help but wonder, "Does God even care?" Yes, He does! In fact, God cares so much, that in 1 Peter 5:7, He said to "Give all your worries and cares to Him, because He cares for you" (NLT). Please don't associate God's silence with Him doing nothing, because He's always up to something. Although you haven't received what you've been praying for, it's not to say you aren't going to get it, but it's simply not time for you to receive it. I don't know the reason for the delay, but I know it must be a good one, if you've waited for so long, which brings me to another issue, time. Not only do we not like to wait, but we don't want to wait an extremely long time.

However, how long is *too* long? Is five years too long to wait? What about one year? Well, it depends upon who you ask, because what you consider to be a long time, can be short to someone else, especially God. Take the incarcerated for example. If that person is sentenced to 25 years in prison for murder, and the person they killed was 28 years of age, what do you think they would say? Obviously, the incarcerated will feel the sentence is too long, but the victim's family will not only say the sentence is not long enough, but the life of the deceased was not long either. You see, 25 years in prison is a long time, but 25 years of life is not nearly long enough. Poor analogy, perhaps, but I'm sure you see my point.

Just because God is making you wait, does not mean he doesn't care about you, so don't think you're not valuable, because you are. You are extremely valuable to Him, because He created you in the likeness of His image. Matthew 6:26 tells us to, "Look at the birds. They don't plant or harvest or store food in barns, for your heavenly Father feeds them. And aren't you far more valuable to Him than they are" (NLT). Of course, you are! You are worth more than petals (flowers) and feathers (birds), so He's not going to allow you to lack and go without. He's Jehovah Jireh, "the God who provides," so you know He's going to provide for you.

I know you've heard the age-old expression, "He might not come when you want Him, but He'll be there right on time," and how many times has He not? I'm sure we'd never have enough "time" to hear your accounts. Although waiting can be difficult, the key is to wait with the expectation that you're going to get what you've prayed to God for. Granted you've been praying for years and don't know when you'll get an answer, but you have the expectation that you'll eventually get what you've been praying for. Matthew 7:7-8 tells us to "Keep on asking, and you will receive what you ask for. Keep on seeking, and you will find. Keep on knocking, and the door will be opened to you. For everyone who asks, receives, everyone who seeks, finds, and to everyone who knocks, the door will be opened" (NLT). I know you've probably asked ninety-nine times, but keep asking, because He might answer on the one-hundredth time.

It's important to have consistent faith, but you need to be persistent as well. I don't care if you sound like a broken record or that annoying child in the grocery store, who keeps asking their mother for candy. It doesn't matter how repetitious you are, just continue to ask! Just because you don't get something when you want it, doesn't mean you're not supposed to have it, or that you should give up. The goal is to stop asking once you get what you've prayed for, not to stop praying, because you haven't received it yet. Be patient and wait on God! Most people can't be patient, because they're too busy looking at what others have, and questioning when it is going to be their time. I'll be the first to admit, I'm notoriously guilty of this.

Anybody that knows me, will tell you my desire to be a wife and mother. I've always dreamt of having identical twins, and when one of my good friends from college became pregnant with twins, not only was I jealous, but I asked God, "When is it going to be my time?" When one of my former colleagues got married to the love of her life, I asked God, "When is it going to be my time?" Although I'm still waiting for it to be my time, I'm glad that God didn't give me what I wanted during the times I asked for them. For one, I was completely unprepared. Two, God knew what I'd experience years later, and if He had blessed me with those things prematurely, it all would've overwhelmed me.

For 20 years, I battled with severe depression and anxiety. God was fully aware of this, and I on the other hand, was completely clueless. He knew there was no way I was prepared to combat a mental illness, tend to a husband and care for 2 newborns, considering the severity of my situation. I want to choose my words carefully, because I don't want anyone, particularly woman, to think you can't live with a mental illness and raise a family, because you absolutely can. In my case, it would've caused my family more harm, than my mental illness did to me. Had things gone according to my plans, I would've collapsed, crawled into a hole, and begged God to get me out! Thankfully, God is much smarter than me.

Like me, a lot of people haven't gotten what they've been praying for, because not only is it not time, but they're not ready. That's why there's such a thing called the "waiting period." During this period, God is developing and preparing you for what's to come. He's not going to allow you to mismanage your blessings, and rather than allow you to fall, He'll just wait for the opportune time. Ecclesiastes 3:1 reminds us that "For everything there is a season, a time for every activity under heaven" (NLT). Again, when it's the right time, you shall receive, but until then, you must continue to have faith and believe. God hears you, He sees you, but most importantly, He wants what's best for you. Whatever you do keep asking, keep seeking Him and don't stop knocking until He opens those doors for you.

When I find myself wanting to cease with my prayer requests, I am reminded of the story in the Gospel of Luke, about a widow, who relentlessly petitioned an unjust Judge for justice. Although he was extremely incompassionate and repeatedly was unwilling to grant her requests, she persisted and consistently asked, because I presume, at some point, she knew he'd have to say yes. If you're familiar with the parable, you know he did eventually render her a yes, but not because he wanted to. More than anything, what he wanted was for her to stop badgering him, and if the only way to get her to stop, was for him to give in, then he gave her what she wanted. Do you see the moral of the story? No matter how many times you're told no, or how long you have to keep asking, the goal is to never stop, until you get what you want.

The widow's situation is probably no different from yours, except she was dealing with an unjust Judge, whereas you're dealing with a Judge who rains on the just as well as the unjust. Like her, you too, must be consistently persistent, and continue to petition God with your requests. It can be daunting at times, and you might even feel as though you're bothering Him, but He'd much rather you give it to Him, than burden yourself and others with it. Besides, if you give your worries to your family and friends, you'll always have them, but if you cast your worries upon God, you'll never have to worry again.

If only you would have listened

I'm not a parent, but I'm pretty sure one of the most difficult things for those who are, is getting their child to listen. To me, repetition is inarguably the first thing a child learns, because it's something that they hear so often. They are constantly told "stop," "sit down," "don't do that," and my all-time favorite word, yet the least effective, "no." It doesn't matter how many times you say the word, the tone you use, or the facial expression to let them know you mean business, your child almost always refuses to listen. You can threaten them with a spanking, timeout, or some form of punishment (i.e. no tv), but they'll continue to do as they have. Yet, once they are in trouble, who is the first person they call on or cry out to? My presumption would be you.

However, can the same not be said about you? How many times have you done something that you know you weren't supposed to have done? How many times has God forewarned you about making a regretful decision, yet you did it anyway? How many times have you been disobedient and not adhered to His word? No doubt it's more times that you can count, and probably care to admit. Like your child, you too called on and cried out to someone, and that someone is God. "I promise, if you'll just get me out of this, I won't do it again," is what you love to say, but don't really mean. Yet and still, you continue to go and do the very thing God asked you not to, and like any other parent, He repeatedly bails you out.

We all can agree, that one of a parent's worst fears is their child getting into trouble. The trouble I'm referring to, is the kind that's easy to get into and incredibly hard to get out. "If only they would have listened," undoubtedly is the common response of mostly all parents, as they try to come up with ways to bail them out, yet again. Proverbs

23:12 says, "Commit yourself to instruction; listen carefully to words of knowledge" (NLT), but do they ever? It's not until they land in hot water or hit rock bottom, that they understand the value of the lesson you were trying to teach them, which would've prevented what's happened.

Sounds familiar? How many times have you hit rock bottom and desperately needed God to pull you out, and He did? God has your best interest at heart. He's not going to tell you to do the right thing, only for you to defy Him and do your own thing. As a parent, you are to protect your children, and God's duty is the same. I can't begin to tell you all the situations I've been in and could've avoided, had I just listened and waited on God. Instead, I chose to do things my way, because I thought I knew what was best for me, when I really didn't. "It's my life and I'm going to live it," was the attitude I had, not knowing it was the reason for most of my problems, although I had foolishly blamed God for them.

However, rather than wait on God, I tried to get ahead of Him. I figured since he wasn't moving fast enough, I should take over for a while. It was way harder than I thought and not at all what I had expected. After the winds became too much that I could withstand, I had no choice but to call on the only one I knew would help me, and like always, He did. I realized I couldn't do God's work, regardless of how hard I try. It didn't matter how many times I tried to run past Him, He always managed to stay ahead. Psalms 119:105 reminds us that, "God's word is a lamp to guide our feet and a light for our path" (NLT). If you're worried, because the path is dark, scary, and never-ending, don't be. Not only is He ahead of you, He's protecting you from behind.

Relieved

Psalms 37:7 encourages us to, "Be still and patiently wait for God to act" (NLT), and that's exactly what I did when I was relieved from my job, in the midst of the Corona pandemic. I was called in for a meeting, and nothing surprised me or caught me off guard, because God had been preparing me for that moment, for a year and three months. What's even more profound, the day prior to my relieve, I called my former colleague and said, "Hey girl, tomorrow I'm going to be let go from my job," to which she replied, "Dee, you're so crazy. How do you know that?" I told her, God had spoken to me that morning and told me, "Tomorrow is it." Of course, she thought I was losing it, but I knew otherwise.

Once I was in my meeting, this person (lacking no genuineness) looked at me and stated, "I feel there is no longer a need for your position, so I've eliminated it." I was unmoved, completely unbothered but more than anything, I was relieved, literally. There was a huge weight lifted off my shoulders, I had never felt freer in my life! I knew that God had closed that door, because another one was about to open. While one would think that I'd lose my mind and question what I was going to do, I was thanking God for what He was about to do. My faith was unshaken, because I knew God was not going to fail me or leave me stranded. He didn't bring me that far, only to leave me. Besides, I was jobless, but not hopeless.

As that door closed, I was at peace and had a joy that was unexplainable, even if I tried to. I was excited, motivated, and ready to start my new journey, because I felt it was going to be my best one yet. I'm thankful to God that He allowed me to serve in that role, because it only prepared me for the biggest role of my life, Entrepreneur. I've always had a desire to start a business, because I wanted something that I could not only call my own but be proud of. I felt so restricted while working for others, and I didn't like the idea of me not possessing any control or having a voice. It was almost as if I were at their mercy and had to do as instructed or else I'd be let go, which ironically, I was.

As a result of my due-diligence and obedience to God, I knew that what was to come, was greater than what was. I've always known in one way or another, that place was not my destination. It was simply a filing station that gave me the experience I needed for my next location. I've never been let go from a job, and neither did I want too, but I knew it was all a part of God's divine plan. Besides, I had tried for a year to leave that job, but nothing ever came through. Even during the times I knew God was telling me to wait, I still proceeded to move. I was desperate and hungry for more, because I felt like there was more to be done. When I have a fervent desire for something, I will stop at nothing until I get it. In order for me to get whatever it is that God has for me, that door had to close. Thankfully, it was an end to that job, but not an end to me.

"What's next?" was the question I was constantly asked. Whenever I'd reply "more," I spoke with such enthusiasm and optimism, because I knew God had great plans for me. In Jeremiah 29:11, God states, "For I know the plans I have for you. They are plans for good and not for disaster, to give you a future and a hope" (NLT). His word is what kept me hopeful and at peace, because I knew God was working things out for my good. That experience really taught me to be still and wait on God. However, that's the issue for a lot of people. They feel as though God isn't moving, but I assure you He is. Sadly, so many people have given up and started to question God and why He's allowing all these tragedies to happen. COVID-19 has taken over, the death toll keeps rising, we're in the middle of a race war, people have lost their jobs, businesses, homes, and the list is never ending. The economy is in complete shambles and my gut tells me, so are you. I hear people say, "If God's plans are for good and not disaster, then why are we in a state of emergency? Why can't He just end this pandemic?" Matthew 26:6 tells us that, "You will be hearing of wars and rumors of wars. See that you are not frightened, for those things must take place, but that is not yet the end" (NLT).

This pandemic has launched a full-on war against the world, but it's not the end of it. I know you want a more concrete answer, but trusting God is the best one I've got. I too, don't understand why things are crumbling before our very eyes, but according to His word in Matthew 26:6, it has too. "Where do we go from here?" is a great question, and the answer is to continue to pray, be patient and wait on God. It's as simple as that, yet so hard for many people to do, including me. They don't have the faith to stand on and the hope to believe that what they ask for, will come to pass. After all, why should they when nothing's happening? Oh, but there is! Just because you can't see God working, doesn't mean that He's not.

The chips are down now, but they won't be much longer. Don't gripe about what you've lost, because God is going to give it back to you and so much more. I'm sure that's the last thing anyone wants to hear, especially when they are at their wicks end. God can move mountains and is capable of restoring things as they were, and even better. He has a plan, and He will *relieve* us from this pandemic. It doesn't take much for you to believe. All you need is faith the size of a mustard seed and leave the rest up to God.

Giant Faith

I'm pretty sure everyone is familiar with the story of David and Goliath. I've heard and read it countless of times, and each time gave me a new meaning. Some of my biggest life experiences have been on the leveling field of David affronting Goliath, but unlike David, I haven't always had the courage to fight, or the faith that I'd win. In 1 Samuel 17:45, David went "before Goliath in the name of the Lord Almighty, the God of the armies of Israel," (NLT). I've always wondered why God couldn't be there for me, as He did David? Truth of the matter, God was always there! Like David, when I realized I didn't need a sword, shield, or army to fight a giant, but instead have giant faith, I knew there wasn't anything I couldn't do, especially without God!

A lot of times, we got it alone, because we feel there's either no choice, or no one to go with us. We tell ourselves, "If I don't do it, then no one else will," when truth of the matter God will do it for us, if only we give our battles to Him. Whenever I was affronted with a giant, I'd say, "God, I can't defeat this thing, but I know you can." Yet, instead of stepping back and allowing Him to fight for me, I'd pick up my sword and shield, not realizing, God is all the armor I need. Although it's tough giving Him something I feel I can handle, it's tougher trying to handle it and then admit that I can't. Yet, I know "I can do all things through Christ, who strengthens me" (Philippians 4:13, NLT).

Just as God has given me strength to fight my way out of many situations I thought for sure I'd lose, He'll give you strength as well. It doesn't matter how big or small your situation is, all you need is faith to believe you're going to overcome. God didn't say your faith had to be the size of your problems, only the size of a mustard seed. Even if you've only got a little amount of faith, it means you've got a lot.

Every step counts

There's nothing more aggravating, than trying to assemble something that's come with a thousand and one pieces. We all dread reading the ever confusing thick "white booklet," also known as the instructions. Before we even allow ourselves the chance to fully read it, let alone follow it, we quickly try to do it on our own. "I got this," we say. A migraine and a few hours later, we're elated and proud of ourselves for completing the assembly. As we try to put it to use, we realize it's not working. We're dumbfounded, because we know, we did everything right, so we're not sure where we went wrong. Although we'd like to think we've dotted every "I" and crossed every "T," we forgot one very important thing, to follow all the steps. Because of our impatience and urgency for wanting things now (and I'm talking right now), we'll skip steps 2-5 to get to 6, when 2-5 are most critical to us. It's during these steps that we learn what we need to complete the process.

Take Moses and the people of Israel, for example. When God gave Moses the decrees and declarations (Ten Commandments), He had Moses to relay to the people of Israel, "You must be careful to obey all commands of the Lord your God, following his instructions in every detail. Stay on the path that the Lord your God has commanded you to follow. Then you will live long and prosperous lives in the land you are about to enter and occupy" (Deuteronomy 5:32-33, NLT). What do you think would've happened, had the people of Israel not obeyed God? Do you think they would've remained where they were, or tried to occupy the land on their own? Most of us can say the latter, because we've tried to do things on our own, a time or two. Instead of following God's command

and waiting for Him, we bypass His instructions, and prematurely make our move, thus resulting in failure.

God has given us a manual (Bible) which serves as a guide to help us in our everyday lives. Let the record reflect, that we're all guilty of not following it for several reasons. Personally, this manual is critical to my entire being, because it not only puts me in position of direct alignment with God and His will for my life, but it keeps me from trying to do His job. I have what I like to call the "takeover spirit," because when I feel as though God is not moving fast enough, I'll take over the situation, only to conclude that I can't do God's work. Psalms 27:14 tells us to, "Wait patiently for the Lord. Be brave and courageous. Yes, wait patiently for the Lord" (NLT). Rather than try and change a situation you have no control over, just hand it over to God. Besides, no matter how many times you give it to Him and take it back, does it ever change your circumstances?

Do you often find yourself hurrying to the next phase, and jumping over steps, because you simply can't wait? Don't worry, we're in this thing together. Take a marriage for example. Typically, before you marry, you go through the dating phase. Here, you learn each other, and share your likes, dislikes, etc. Next, (if all goes well) you meet what could possibly be your best friend or your worst enemy, the family. At this point, you're about to determine if you're going to run to the altar or for your life. All jokes aside, this step is important, because if you're planning a future with someone, you want to know what you're getting yourself into. Once you pass this step, you think it's smooth sailing, until you encounter a riptide, commonly called living together. This is important for a lot of people, because they want to know if they are able to coexist with their partner, if they're clean, leave the seat up, and so forth. In other words, do I really want to marry you?

Many people would argue that these are minor things they can tolerate, but why adopt an intolerable attitude when it comes to God? It behooves me to know that people will wait all day for a particular person's phone call, wait to hear back from a company they've applied to work for, wait for an acceptance letter from college, wait in a ridiculously long line for a pair of sneakers, but refuse to wait on God. Is the fulfillment and joy you receive from the aforementioned things, far greater than what you can receive from God? I'm sure one would much rather stand in line for an hour or two, as opposed to waiting on God, because it seems that most times, it takes forever for Him to respond. However, you can't put a timeline on God. Possibly, could it be that He is "taking so long," because you still aren't where He needs you to be?

Preparation occurs for a number of reasons. It helps builds our faith in God. It strengthens us, causes us to be more patient, and it helps us to maintain our blessings. which leads me to question, "Are you prepared?" Do you think you're ready and have what it takes? Although a lot of people will make it here, they won't stay. When they moved without God and skipped steps 2-5, they failed to get what's required to not only help them reach step 6, but to stay there. You should know that this is particularly not about marriage, and probably not the best analogy, but I can only hope you see what I'm trying to convey. Be patient and wait on God to move! It's so easy to become antsy and want to rush to the next level in our lives, so much so, you end up skipping the line, when you needed to wait your turn. Remember, every step counts, so please take your time and wait on God!

Out of alignment

Many, many years ago, I, along with some family members, were in a bad car accident. We were injured and pretty sore but thank God I survived to tell it. Some days following, if not a week, I had to go to a Chiropractor for therapy. My neck was stiff and sore, and I could barely move it, but my back required the most attention. I can remember very vividly, a constant burning sensation, followed by pain, which started from the top of my shoulders, moved down my spine, and ended at the lower part of my back. In other words, my back was bent out of shape and required realignment.

I was reluctant to go, because I could barely tolerate the pain, let alone being put through more. I'll admit, I was not a happy camper, because those sensory treatments I received, felt like thousands of tiny ants eating away at my back. I had to frequently use cold compress packets, and although they gave me relief, they didn't give me what I needed. This continued for weeks, and once complete, I was thankful to resume my normal activities, and the adjustment to my back, was just what I needed. Just think, had I not been realigned, I probably wouldn't be able to stand up straight or sit down without discomfort.

I love storytelling, and although you might question the need for this one, let me tell you the moral of it. When we are out of alignment with what God has called us to do, we will experience pain and discomfort. It can last for weeks, months, and years even, but until we do what we're required to do, the longer it'll take for God to give us relief. If you're tired of your life being bent out of shape, and you want to get over the hump, God is the perfect adjustor! Get into alignment and watch Him move!

A different agenda

For two years, I practically begged this well-known Editor, to allow me to not only write a post for her column, but to become a permanent Staff Writer on the team. I'd given her samples of my work (my best work at that) and still, no response. I know one would think, after a few months' time or a year even, they'd give up, but I couldn't. I kept on asking and being persistent, because eventually it'd pay off, right? Needless to say, it did! I started *Notes by La'Rue* in November 2018, in one of my favorite spots on earth, Starbucks. As I was crying (literally) and asking God why she wouldn't allow me to write for her column, He gave me the idea to create something that He wanted, and others so desperately needed. The agenda was the same, but the only difference, it was on my platform instead of hers.

To think, I was going to give up writing, because I thought no one found me interesting, nor did they want to read what I had to say. Due to my impatience, I reached out to other columnists, somehow praying, and hoping they'd give me a chance. However, God granted me the space I needed to do what I do best, which is motivate, encourage, and inspire. I know I am more than skilled, gifted, and capable of writing, so it was never a question as to whether or not I couldn't, but why someone wouldn't acknowledge it. I understand everyone has their own preference and style, and maybe, mine was not hers. I hold no grievances or resentment towards the young lady, and I even support her column. Creating my blog has been one of the best things that could've happened to me, and others too. One thing I have learned, is that we're so quick to add to someone else's success, when God wants us to have our own.

There's nothing wrong with helping others, but sometimes God will intervene, because He has a different (and better) agenda than the one we have for ourselves. After two years of blogging, I'll admit, it has been fairly hard to obtain followers and get my likes up, but God reminded me it's not about me, but His people. It's about Him using me as a vessel to draw others near to Him, with the hopes that they'd soon seek Him for themselves. To be honest, since God has changed my life for the better, I've always aspired for others to see Him in me, and ultimately want a relationship with Him. I try to inform them that their relationship with God is not going to look like mine, nor should they try to copy it. My dealings with God are completely different from others, and while we all may experience some of the same situations or hardships, what God does for me is not necessarily what He would do for someone else, and vice versa.

It's not to say that I'm preferred or better than anyone else, but I do know that I'm favored. Besides, what God has for me, is strictly for me, and the same applies for others. I can't have what belongs to you, because it's not mine to keep. Looking back, imagine some of the things you set your sight on to do, and when things didn't go according to plan, or your plan I should say, you gave up. You've probably figured things weren't meant to be, so you question the need to keep trying. However, God's word tells us to "Keep knocking and the door shall be opened unto you." I can't begin to tell you how many years I've knocked and knocked, and no one ever answered. However, I waited on God and stood on His word and continued to knock, because I knew at some point, the door would eventually open, and it did. Be persistent, wait on God, but whatever you do, keep on knocking. Eventually, the door of opportunity is going to open for you. Just be patient, and you'll be glad that you did.

Now is not the time

I want to be married, right now! I want a set of identical twin girls, right now! I want my house built from the ground up, right now! I want to cut the ribbon for the grand opening of my business, CH1 Bookstore and Lounge, right now! There are so many things I want "right now," but *now* is not the time! Ecclesiastes 3:1 tells us, "For everything there is a season, a time for every activity under the sun" (NLT), and when the time is right, it'll happen. Not just a little bit, but all of it! When it comes to things I want or would like to do, my pursuit is undeniably fervent.

Being eager is a good thing, and it's also my problem. I can't stay where I'm at long enough to enjoy what I have or get what I need, because I'm always on the move. "I've got to move, because God isn't, and if I don't act now, the opportunity won't come again." Yet, if it's mine, it won't miss me or pass me by. When I feel as though He's not moving fast enough, I intervene and try to speed up the process, but He always brings me to a complete standstill, and I can't stand that! Don't you see, I can't afford to stop? If I do, it'll delay my mission, but if I don't, God will abort it.

So, I might as well just wait. Besides, I can't accelerate until He releases the brake. It's a good thing He didn't, because who knows what would've happened. How can He take you to the next level, when you can't get passed the one you're on? Everybody wants God to do this for them and that for them, but they can't sit still long enough to wait for Him to do it. What you need to do, is get out of the fast lane and into your lane, because you can't keep up with others. Life is not a race, so you can't run with the masses, expecting to get ahead. When it's time for you to go, you will, but now is not the time. Just be still and wait on God's timing.

Beautiful timing

Majority of my notes are reoccurring, when it comes to being still and waiting on God. I'm intentionally repetitive, but it's only because I'm trying to convince and help you, and myself too. While I do believe what I put out, it can be really hard to take it in. Oddly, I've always been great at inspiring and building others up but struggle to keep myself afloat. Although I consider myself to be Superwoman, I also know when I need to be saved. Whether the rescue is financial, mental, physical, or emotional, we all can benefit from some help every once in a while. Yet sometimes, the most difficult thing is waiting for the help to arrive. Granted God won't show up when we'd like Him to, Ecclesiastes 3:11 gives us comfort in knowing, "God has made everything beautiful for its own time" (NLT).

You may get tired of me saying the same things over and over again, and you may be beyond tired of waiting, but it doesn't matter how many times I say it, or how long you wait, just know that when it does happen, it'll be the most perfect and beautiful time. This message is not just for you, but me as well. Rest assured, I'm not just giving notes, I'm taking them too! When you feel you can't go any further or want to give up, always refer back to your notes, but most importantly, ask God for His strength. Remember, when we are weak, He is strong. If it helps, Jacob worked for 7 years to receive Rachel. It took Noah almost 100 years to build the Ark. It took Hannah more than 90 years to become pregnant with Samuel. It took 7 days for the walls of Jericho to fall down. It took God 6 days to create the earth, and you can't even wait a minute?

Although years would pass before either of these biblical characters could see God's promise, they didn't lose faith. Isaiah 40:31 tells us, "They that wait on the Lord, shall renew their strength. They shall mount up with wings, just like an eagle and soar. They shall run and not be weary. They shall walk and never faint" (NLT). All you have to do is wait on His timing! It may seem as though it's taken forever to receive an answered prayer, and others such a short amount of time, but all you see is what they have. What you didn't see, was how long it took them to get it. Just think, if God can create the earth in 6 days, can you imagine how fast He can answer your prayers? Keep seeking. Keep knocking. Keep asking. Yet most of all, keep faithfully waiting!

Wait on the promise

I don't know which is worse, waiting on something to happen or waiting on someone to *make* it happen. Either way, I can be pretty anxious at times and hate to be kept waiting, especially if it's longer than two hours. The uncertainty of whether or not I'll get what I want hovers over my head like an aircraft, but when I look up and see who's flying, my doubts start to wither away. In past situations, I've moved too quickly, when I all I needed to do was slow down and be still. Besides, my hastiness never got me anywhere. I've learned all too well, that if what you are seeking to do is not of God's will, then it won't get done. It doesn't matter how bad you want it or how much you petition God for it, if He didn't promise it, you won't receive it. Regardless of whatever it is, sometimes it's best that we don't get it.

Can you imagine being in a leadership role, but not knowing how to lead? You've never governed over an entity, yet you think you have what it takes to do it. I thought I could be President of one of the local Community Colleges in my state, so I applied for the position. I figured since I had worked in the collegiate system for 13 years and knew the ins and outs of the educational system, I could manage being President. Although I've overseen the daily operations of a department, I didn't have the first clue on how to maintain a budget, other than my personal bank account, and I can barely do that right. Sure, I was a leader, team player and all the other qualities one would normally look for when hiring their ideal candidate. However, I had no experience with making organizational financial decisions, establishing, and maintaining donor funding, and strategic planning to name a few. I've never really had to create a strategic plan, because I always operated off of the one that was in existence. Needless to say, I was still hopeful and optimistic that I would get the job, because I felt that it was what God was leading me to do. Turns out, God was leading me to be patient and wait on Him.

I'm pretty sure you have already concluded that I didn't get the job. Not only did I not get the job, I didn't even get an interview. I'll be honest, I was fairly disappointed, because like all the other times, I was for certain that this was it. When I didn't get the position, I murmured to God, "This can only mean you have something way better for me. However, I need you to understand that, that job was paying six figures." I was reminded that although the job offered a wonderful salary, God could (and would) put me in a position to earn substantially more. My focus shifted from disappointment to joy, because I knew where God was about to take me, but I just didn't know when. That's where a lot of people lose sight of what they're trying to obtain, because they don't expect to get it. They've become impatient and discouraged thinking it's never going to happen, because it hasn't happened yet. Could it be that it hasn't taken place, because God is still putting you in a place of position to receive it?

When God makes a promise, it doesn't come back void, and He has to honor what He's promised. When God made a promise to Abraham, He didn't rescind it. Galatians 3:17 tells us that, "The agreement God made with Abraham could not be canceled 430 years later when God gave the law to Moses. God would be breaking His promise" (NLT). We all know that God is not a man that He would lie, so He has to honor His word. You shouldn't worry about what hasn't happened but instead prepare for when it does happen. Live with the expectation that God will answer and stop expecting the worst. God is faithful and His promises are still good. Everything will happen within God's perfect timing. All you've got to do is wait on Him to fulfill the promise.

Change of plans

When I was in Undergraduate school, my career plans were to become an Attorney, so I majored in Political Science. Although I am not "into" politics, I wanted to be a Prosecutor, so I could put the bad guys (and girls) away, not to mention, make a lot of money. Nearing the end of completing my degree, I realized, that's not what I wanted to do. I thought, "Are you kidding me?" I can't tell you how many times I've asked myself that, considering the fact that I had just gone through four years of college and accrued financial debt, only to "discover" I desired a different career. I was disappointed, to say the least, because I felt all the money and time I invested into attending college, was a total waste, although I'd later learn it was not.

Seeing that Law School and teaching a high school Government class was out of the question, I then questioned, "What is it that I absolutely love, am good at it, and I know I can do?" I think you all know the answer to that. Although I never made it into the courtroom, I made it to a place where I am most happy, writing! When you're younger, you're almost forced to have your career plans all figured out, and sometimes, people have already done it for you. Nowadays, people rarely get to live out their dreams, because they're too busy living out someone else's. When I worked in higher education, I can't begin to tell you how many young ladies came to school to be a Nurse, because it was what their mom wanted them to do. I'd then reply, "But what do you want to do?"

I'm sure you can imagine the number of disgruntled looks I encountered, but those student's happiness overrode their parent's intrusive decision making. If only parents, or anyone for that matter, knew the disservice and harm they are causing, all for the sake of their child having the perfect job. No doubt, they have depression too, because they are not happy doing what they love. Often times, I wonder where I'd be now had I gone to Law School, and my thoughts are still the same, financially independent, but miserable.

Have you ever wanted to do something, but when the time came, there was a complete change of plans? Ironically, isn't that what God does? He'll sit and let us form these big plans and watch us attempt to go through with them. No matter what we do, nothing manages to go right. We pray to God, pleading and asking for His help, but He doesn't bulge. You just have to be patient and wait on what God is going to do for you, instead of you trying to do things on your own. We can't always have things our way, and honestly, I'm glad that we don't. I can't begin to imagine the hurt and pain God has kept us from. There are so many people and things He's protected us from, to which we know nothing about. All we know is, we want to live our lives the way we please. Yet the lives we lead are not pleasing to Him.

Although I knew being an Attorney is what I wanted, I just knew it was not what I was supposed to be doing. Everything that I've done, has given me a sense of fulfillment. I've always felt as though I have a purpose, although it took me a long time to figure it out. My purpose is to use my gift of writing and speaking to motivate, inspire and help people all over the world, while leading them to Christ. Every day, I'm happy, because I get the chance to do that. Even though we may have our own set of plans, God always has something bigger in mind, because typically, we think too small. You might prefer your plans over His, but His plans are always better. Jeremiah 29:11 states, "For I know the plans I have for you, declares the Lord. Plans to prosper you and not harm you. Plans to give you hope and a future" (NLT). I'm not sure about you, but I don't think my plans (or yours) can get any better than His.

Waiting to say I do

I've had some of the absolute worst luck when it comes to dating, so much so, my love life is pretty nonexistent. I've always been the woman who dreams, fantasizes, and idolizes her wedding day, and there are times I wonder if I'll ever have one. I can remember watching Cinderella as a little girl, wishing that I was she. In some ways, we're actually a lot alike. We both are beautiful, were poor, mistreated and not well-liked by people. Although she didn't have a good life (neither did I), in the end she married her Prince Charming, and lived happily ever after. Yet here I am at the age of 37, still waiting to say I do. I know some of you are probably questioning my sanity while reading or feel as though I "have my whole life ahead of me," but I feel as though I'm running out of time. I'm not sure if I can attribute my hurriedness to societies time standards or my own impatience, but either way, I'm ready to be a wife.

I'm what you would consider a hopeless romantic, and no matter how unlucky I've been to find it, I'm still anxiously awaiting "the one." In fact, I've been so anxious to wed, that I've almost risked it all, just to walk down that isle. I convinced myself that two of the guys I was involved in, were the one, but God was telling (and showing) me otherwise. Rather than follow what God placed on my heart to do, I allowed my mind to overrule Him. Regardless of their backgrounds, I gave them the benefit of the doubt, because I know what it's like to be held hostage to your past, so I didn't want to judge them just as I'd been. The first man I disobeyed God for, not only robbed me of my time, but my self-esteem and peace of mind. God had shown me repeatedly, that He wasn't the one, but I boldly told God, He wasn't the one to make that decision for me. As a result, I paid for it dearly. There was no abuse of any kind, but I'm sure you know what it's like when you're parents told you to stay away from a certain guy, only for you to rebel, and wished you had of listened. Sadly, six years passed, before I finally "got the message" God had been conveying.

The second man, on the other hand, looked like my Prince Charming, but in hindsight, I actually should've looked the other way. He seemed like such a sweet, charismatic, and caring gentleman. We both had come from similar backgrounds, with regards to living in poverty and having an absentee dad. The connection was almost instant, and before you knew it, we were "best friends." Although our friendship raised several eyebrows, the objections didn't raise any alarms with me. In case you're wondering, this man is imprisoned. Trust me, I know. Your reaction is now mine, as I grimace while telling this story. If I'm completely honest, I can't even tell you how I ended up in the situation, but I had no clue down the line, I'd be begging God to let me out. For months, we talked on the phone and wrote letters, and even began to plan what would happen next, once he was released, but as God would have it, He quickly abrupted those plans (and thank God he did)!

As I mentioned earlier, he was very charismatic (most con artist are), but deep down inside, I knew something wasn't quite right about him. Seeking to prove myself wrong and discredit my heart, I continued to engage with him. As a side note, ladies, and gentlemen, please listen to and follow your heart. We've all heard the expression, "A mind is a terrible thing to waste" but following it can get you in trouble at times. You'll understand why later as the story unfolds. To continue, things were pretty good in the beginning, and although I took no issues with him or anything he said, my skepticism continued to lurk behind. As time passed, things gradually went from good to great, until the smoke alarm begin to siren. Immediately, I felt the sudden urge to run, but my mind kept me in place. It assured me that it was a false alarm, and shortly thereafter, everything resumed to normal.

Fast forwarding, while we too, were moving fast, I felt the need to slow things down. In fact, I wanted them to come to a halt, because the person I met, was far from the one I had suddenly been introduced to. He started to ask me for money, accused me of not helping him to be paroled, and even blamed everyone for his sentence or not wanting to see him released, when in fact he was the sole reason for his incarceration. There he was "desperately fighting to get out and live his life," yet the one he took, would never be again. I was completely flabbergasted and offended even, and often expressed my frustrations with his way of thinking, but I still never judged him. I tried to help him see things with a different and better prospective. Prior to his tantrums, I'd try to console and lift him up with prayer, but after a while the devil has to eventually show you why he was casted out in the first place, which is what he did. After months of hearing this, you'd think I'd have had enough, but I continued to be his friend.

Innately, I'm a caring person and try to see the good in people, but there wasn't anything good inside of that man, once the veil was removed. Everything was no fault of his own, and always someone else's doing. He was still harboring resentment, anger, and frustration with the world, but God mainly, when he was responsible for his own choices, and not willing to affront his demons. By now, I'm looking for an exit, although God had warned me not to enter to begin with. As I was making my way out, I slowly cut off our communication and ceased to send (or receive) any more letters. Immediately, he started to question why I wasn't answering his calls and who I was talking to. At that point, his "visitation hours" were officially over! From his ugly attitude, un-Christian like spirit, to the low language he used, I witnessed it all! God had not only given me a front row seat to the real him, He spoke to me in my dreams, and gave me visions of this man physically assaulting me. God repeatedly said, "This is what I was trying to get you to see all along.

Throughout this whole ordeal, I had been speaking to you through your heart, and tried to change your mind, but you just wouldn't listen. It took me using this situation to hurt you, just so you could walk away." Whew! Talk about being chastened by God. I was very much hurt by the situation, but more than anything, I was hurt that I didn't listen to and wait on God. Whether or not you know it or believe it, God speaks to us through our heart (Hebrews 4:13), and the enemy through our mind. Anytime you have negative, harmful, evil, doubtful, hopeless, or low thoughts, listen to your heart, because it makes it impossible to hear the enemy. You may feel like the man/woman that you are with is not the one, but your mind will say, "Everyone is already married, and you're still waiting to say I do. Do it, or you'll be single and lonely forever." However, just because you aren't married, doesn't mean it won't happen.

All of those people you know who are married and "pretending" to be happy, might be like me, looking for a way out. Either they thought he/she was the one, rushed and married prematurely, or their self- worth was so low, they thought the only way to pick it up again, was if they had someone to do it for them. Contrary to what you might have seen or heard, no one can make you feel good about you, but you! A man/woman doesn't complete you, make you whole, nor are they responsible for your happiness. A lot of times, we look for others to make us happy, and when they don't, we misplace the blame on them. I used to think, "Oh, I'll be so glad when I meet and marry my husband, because I know he's going to make me so happy." I'd gotten so fed up with not being able to fully love myself, that I was now choosing to allow someone else to do it for me. However, I can assure you of this, it doesn't matter how much someone else loves you, because if you don't love yourself, how they feel about you will soon become a matter of question.

You won't be able to accept or believe that their love is real, because you don't really love yourself, and can't imagine someone else being able to either. I'm not sure if you've had a traumatic life, was neglected, or not shown love when you were a child or have been in some pretty unhealthy, and unfortunate relationships, but no matter what you've experienced, please don't allow it to reshape how you feel about yourself. More than anything, I want you to be confident and love the man/woman you are, or are becoming, because when you're content with self and aware of who you are and whose you are, you won't feel the need to wait for someone to make you happy or feel good. I can promise you this, it's a wonderful feeling being able to love yourself. It took me going to therapy to bring to light, the things I couldn't see or accept about myself. Now that I realize that self-love is greater than any love I can receive, I won't look for a man to trump it.

I'm not sure where you are in the process of waiting to be wed, but don't allow someone else's fairytale ending, to question if you'll ever get your own. No matter what your family, friends, or society say, you're not running out of time. Only God knows your time, and if He didn't say "it's time," then you need to get into position and wait. If you're in an unhealthy relationship, and you've been warned by God, given red flags, or have heard the smoke alarm, you need to be like Usain and quickly bolt! Don't let what someone else's perception of what your life should like, cause you to have an unhappy one. Striving to have someone else's relationship shouldn't be one of your "goals" either. People will try their best to make their relationship look good to you, and turn around to sell you a dream, that they're still waiting to come true.

Don't believe the hype! So many people rush to say, "I do," when they should've waited on God to do better. I'd been warned by my family, but I kept trying to convince myself, things are not as they make them seem. Trust me, they are. Maya Angelou famously said, "When a person shows you who they are believe them." I don't care how sweet they talk to you, the gifts they give, or how good-looking they are, the minute you feel something is not right, is normally the right time to leave. I felt so worthless towards the end of my friendship with that man, and even questioned my integrity. I make no admission that I am better than him, but clearly could've done way better by waiting on God.

Don't lose your self-esteem or self-worth behind a man/woman, you were never intended to be with. There were times I put my friendship with him, before my relationship with God, to which I would never do again. When you think you're in love, you'll often find yourself doing some silly and regretful things. Understandably, I have major regret, feelings of anger and resentment. The funny thing is, I don't know who I'm angrier at, him or myself. I sometimes sit and question, "How could he do this to me?" It's not long before I realize the question is for myself. I now realize that if only I'd cared enough about myself, I could've saved a lot of time and pain. While I'd like to think giving it to him was all a complete waste, I know it never was.

As cliché as it sounds, that situation not only made me a better person, it made me understand that God cares so deeply about me, He wasn't going to allow me to risk my life, for the sake of being just "anybody's" wife. I don't care how desperate you are to wed, be still and wait on God to send you your kingdom spouse. You might feel like you've been waitlisted, but He hasn't forgotten about you. If Sarah can wait until she's 90 years old to be a mother, and Abraham 105 years to be a father, you can certainly wait on God. I promise you, He has someone better for you, so don't settle. Once you see who God has reserved for you, you're going to be glad that you did wait.

Driven in a different direction

As I previously mentioned, when I was younger, I've always dreamt of becoming an Attorney. I wanted so desperately to be a Prosecutor, so I could get the bad people off the street, not to mention, I am a great debater. Once I graduated from high school, I made plans to go to college to pursue my dreams. I enrolled at Tuskegee University and majored in English. Obviously, writing is my first love and greatest passion, and although English is an excellent field of study, I felt it wouldn't give me the edge I needed to get into Law School. After my first semester, I not only changed my major, but I changed schools as well. I decided to attend Troy University that winter semester, and there I majored in Political Science, and later obtained both my Bachelor's and Master's degree. Granted, I didn't know the first thing about politics, yet I figured it couldn't be too hard to learn.

I was intrigued to learn of the Judicial system, but the closer I got to the end of my degree requirements, my dreams of becoming an Attorney started to change. I didn't understand why, because I had dreamt of this my whole life, and I was literally months away from taking the LSAT and getting into Jones School of Law. While shaking off the idea of not attending law school, I bought every book possible to help me prepare for the LSAT and paid my fee to secure a testing spot. I was ready to take that exam, but God wasn't. In fact, He didn't even allow me too. Instead, He shifted my focus from the court room back into the classroom. "God, what are you doing?" I asked, because this is not what I had planned for my life. I argued, I wanted to be a Prosecutor, not a Counselor. Besides, what was I going to do with that degree? Was I to counsel the bad guys, so they could stay out of trouble, I sarcastically presumed? Whatever God's reasoning, I knew it was good, although I didn't understand.

Rather than attend Law School, I went to Graduate School to pursue a career in Counseling and Psychology. Still unsure, I continued to follow God's lead. As cliché as it sounds, my mission in life was always to be able to help people through whatever circumstances they were facing. I begin to wonder, how would I apply that to Law School. Even though I'm a compassionate person, the goal wasn't to express feelings of empathy, but to enforce the law, and let criminals know if they break them, there are repercussions. Have you ever sat and thought about the repercussions you'd suffer, if you broke God's law? What do you suppose life would look like for you?

2 Chronicles 31:21 tells us that, "In all that he did in the service of the Temple of God and in his efforts to follow God's *laws and command*, Hezekiah sought his God wholeheartedly. As a result, he was very successful" (NLT). I'm not sure about you, but I want to be extremely successful. That's not to say that if we break God's law, He won't bless us. Surely He will, because He offers forgiveness, something most of us find hard to do for others and ourselves. In any event, I followed God's command and completed Graduate School in the spring of 2012. From there, I continued to work at the school, but there was a position that came open, that I had initially resisted, but later applied for. One of the many requirements of the position, was for the candidate to have a Master's degree in Counseling and Psychology. Go figure! It all made sense to me, and God was making a way for me.

Not only that, He knew what that department needed, and I was going to be the one to give it to them. Granted it was no easy fete, but by God's grace and mercy, I was able to do exactly what He had called me to do, help others through their circumstances. Besides, that was my whole agenda anyway. From time to time, I still think what would've happened had I not obeyed God. Who knows where that path would've led me to, but God knows, that's why He didn't allow me to take it. It's easy to encounter unforeseeable circumstances, especially when we can't see them. However, God can see way farther than we can, so He already knows what's ahead. Rather than allow you to do something that could potentially have a negative impact on your life, He'll drive you in a different direction.

The question is, "Are you willing to follow His lead?" "He knows the plans He has for you. Plans to prosper you and not harm you. Plans to give you hope and a future" (Jeremiah 29:11, NLT). I know this is your third time reading this verse, so take it as your confirmation, God's plans are always better than the ones we have for ourselves. It may not be what you want to do, but He has a reason for everything. It doesn't matter what you want to do in life or who you aspire to be, if it's not a part of God's plan, He'll derail you to the way in which you're supposed to go.

You may be driving to the place of your dreams, but if you are steered to go another way, trust God's direction, and follow along. A lot of times, we may think we are cruising to our desired destination, when we could very well be headed towards a dead end. Wherever He's taking you, you might experience a few delays, setbacks, and roadblocks, but no matter how long it takes you to get there, you'll reach your destination right on time. There's no need to speed, just wait and follow God's lead.

Traveling through impossible circumstances

"I'm tired, and I just can't do this anymore!" Would you believe me if I told you, you could? Probably not, considering the fact that your circumstances have somehow convinced you that it's the "end of the world." However, I'm here to tell you that it's not! I talk a lot about adversity, hardships, and struggles, and it's because I've been met with them more times than I'd care to acknowledge, and you'd like to read. However, although my journey has been tough, one thing that I vowed never to do, was to stop going, regardless of how bad the circumstances were. Besides, if you give up, how will you ever know whether or not things will get better? Like me, you've been through plenty of challenging situations, and are probably still entangled in some. Granted, they absorbed all of your energy and took a toll on you mentally, emotionally, and physically, but you eventually got through them, right?

One of the things I appreciate most about traveling through impossible circumstances, is no matter how many obstacles I encounter, I know that if I see them as an opportunity for challenge and growth, instead of a roadblock, it increases my chances of actually overcoming them. Remember the age-old expression, "Nothing is impossible, because the word alone says, "I'm possible." Our trials and tribulations have worn us thin and made it too easy to give up and quit. As a result of all the dangerous curves and rocky roads we've driven, we'll pull over and question God whether or not we should continue to drive or turn around and go back. However, just as He's brought you through the trenches before, He'll do it again. Every drive is not going to be smooth, and you're bound to run into some potholes and traffic, but it doesn't matter what you go through or how impossible things may look, keep going. God's behind you!

Can't hardly wait

Sometimes I can't stand the fact that I'm so "impulsive," as one of my former students so kindly put it. "Ms. B., sometimes I feel like you don't have any patience with us, because you seem to be in a hurry a lot," was the words she boldly said to me. For once, I didn't argue, because I can be in a bit of a "rush" at times. I tend to treat life as a relay race, hoping and praying, to make it across the finish line, but it's the waiting to cross that makes me so anxious. Although the process can be lengthy, it's during that time we are being pruned and prepped for what awaits us next. I have a lot of dreams and goals that I've yet to fulfill, and I often question if I'll ever. I'm very proactive and don't necessarily appreciate down time, so I'm almost always busy. Once I complete a project, I quickly thrust myself into another one, because I figured that God won't bless me if He sees that I'm not trying, or perhaps I'm trying a little too much?

However, I can't afford to slack, for if I do, it'll only extend the process longer. So, how does one know how long it's going to be? Only God knows that, but one thing I do know is, I can't hardly wait until I'm finally where I want to be, but what if it's not where God places me? Everyone can make their own plans, but if it's not in God's plan, it won't happen. It's not to say that you can't have dreams and aspirations, so don't ever stop having those. Place yourself in a position to hear from God and seek His will for your life. Yes, it's a process, which entails waiting, but it'll be worth it in the end. I've learned a valuable lesson, and it's when I can't hardly wait for something and try to rush my way through, I often end up not getting the outcome I desperately wanted. Sometimes, the best thing we can do is be still and wait on God to move.

Detours

I remember being in church one Sunday morning, and the Pastor said, "Your problems have an expiration date and won't last always." That resonated with me, because it was in that very moment that I realized, all that I was going through would be over with soon, but I just didn't know how soon. I had encountered a many roadblocks and didn't know how I was going to go around them, or if I would. Credit card bills were piling up, I wasn't making any money, I was looking for my own place, and quitting my job seemed like the easiest thing to do at that point. Besides, I no longer enjoyed what I was doing.

After graduating from college and eventually post-secondary school, I began my quest to find a career. Application after application, I received denials or simply didn't get a call back. Although I was rejected by those companies, I continued to apply for other jobs. My faith had become smaller than the size of a mustard seed, so that should tell you it was non-existent. I was so tired of hearing "no" or "we appreciate your interest," to the point I wanted to call it quits. Despite not ever hearing from anyone, I continued in my pursuit of happiness. I'll admit, after a while, my faith really started to waiver, because I felt as though God had forgotten about me or was punishing me.

Little did I know, God wasn't punishing me. He forced me to take a slight detour, because the route I had chosen for myself was not what God wanted, nor would it take me to where He wanted me to be. While on this detour, I drove down the "road to change," traveled a little on "new attitude boulevard," and managed to even cruise on "positive avenue," all the things I needed to get me around my roadblocks. Realization had set in, and I knew that in order for me to walk straight into God's will and purpose, I had to do some things I hadn't done before or was willing to do. I had to climb over quite a few walls, jump over many hurdles and open a lot of closed doors, especially ones that people told me couldn't be opened.

Suddenly, my problems didn't overwhelm me anymore, because I knew God was bigger than them and would help me overcome them. As my life began to lead me to more detours, I reached places I'd never thought I'd see, encountered people who helped me get through my problems and became a better woman. My life changed for the best and the problems I thought would last for eternity, had expired. It was then I played back the invisible tape recorder of the words the Pastor had spoken previously, "Your problems have an expiration date and won't last forever." I can smile now, because I know he was right, although I couldn't see it in the beginning. I want you to know that no matter how bad or difficult your situation is, it's not going to be that way forever.

It may seem like it's taking an eternity for things to get better, or you may feel as though God is not listening. I've felt your pain. There were so many times I cried out to Him and accused Him of leaving me when I needed Him most, but we know the word alone tells us, "He'll never leave you nor forsake you." Besides, He's Emmanuel, which translates to, "God with us." Sometimes, our wait can be longer than expected, because God is waiting for us to take the first step, while we expect Him to walk the entire way for us. Stop traveling roads that are familiar to you or offer you a sense of security. God has already gone before you, so He knows what awaits you ahead. It's going to take you making a detour every once in a while, in order for you to end up on the path God has chosen for you. When He steers the wheel of your life, trust Him, and make the turn.

Transportation problems

One of my friends, who I'm very fond of, shared an inspirational story with me, during one of my seasons of difficulty. She knew I hadn't been feeling my best, and wanted to give up, but the story made me reconsider. The jiffs of it, tells why people don't like to be uncomfortable during seasons of uncertainty, and the things they have to endure to get to their destination. It continued by stating that our trials and tribulations, is the method God uses to transport us from one area of our lives to the next. After reading the message, I smiled, became a little tearful, angry, but then relieved. I realized what I had gone through was temporary, but my longsuffering made me think it was permanent. Although I was happy, I was emotional and quite upset with God, because I didn't like the "travel" plans He gave me. I have experienced the absolute worst transportation troubles in my life, starting from childhood.

I've traveled through poverty, homelessness, and being unemployed, and although I know there was a better way for me to come out of the three, God had me to go the way I did for a reason. Whatever that reason is, I'm not sure, and will never know. Since I'm so used to driving and being in charge, I figured this was God's way of telling me He had to "take the wheel," because I had veered off course one too many times. I sometimes still find myself sitting in the passenger seat, with my arms fold, starring out the window, all the while asking, "Are we there yet?" This has been a very long journey and uncomfortable ride, but I know sooner than later, I'm going to awake to God's voice saying, "We're here!" Your ride may be long, bumpy, and come to a stop at times, but it won't be long before you get to where you're supposed to be! Keeping riding and keep trusting God!

Hold on, it'll get better

I talk to God a lot! Almost to the point, I have to preface and say, "I know we just talked, but I forgot to tell you something." Am I the only one that finds humor in that? Maybe so, but that's just my personality. I'm always asking God for something, and if that's not enough, I always say to Him, "Please do it for me and You don't have to wait until the end of the year to do it." I know, the gall of me. However, I am bold with my requests, because Hebrews 4:16 tells us to, "Come boldly and confidently into the throne of our gracious God. There we will receive His mercy, and we will find grace to help us when we need it most" (NLT). I'm not sure about you, but I need Him all the time, so I constantly seek His wisdom and blessings.

Aside from writing, one of my other passions (and God-given gifts) is motivational speaking. I love talking (sometimes a little too much) and speaking with people. It doesn't matter if it's one person or five hundred, I want to talk, because God always give me a message to relay. Although, I am a people person and extrovert, I have introverted characteristics, which causes me to crave my space and alone time. Whenever I pray to God, I always ask that He uses me in a way to not only help others, but to positively impact their lives. Little did I know, one of the most pivotal moments in my life was to about to come forth. For months, I asked this company to allow me to speak with their students and to purchase my books. A lady who attended my first book signing and who just so happens to work for the company, told me she wanted me to do a presentation to the students and that they would purchase my books. Of course, I was elated. However, that joy would soon turn to sadness.

Not only did she not make good on her word, she never made mention of it again. I was hurt, to say the least, but what I couldn't understand, was why would someone not want to help me, especially if it's within their power to do so. I later learned that she didn't help me, because she was jealous of my gift, and how well-received I was by others. In other words, she hated the way other people loved me and spoke so highly of me. That was no reason to not afford me an opportunity, but it was every reason for her to try and keep me stagnant. However, we all know that what the devil meant for bad, God will turn it around for our good, and He did!

After months of trying to convince her, God presented me with an offer of a lifetime. As a result of giving one of my former Supervisor's a copy of my book, he in turn gave it to his Supervisor, and she invited me to speak to a group of high school students that her company had partnered with. They were extremely generous to me, and God was more than good to me, because He not only gave me a chance to speak, but a chance to make a positive impact in the lives of those young adults. That experience was one of my most euphoric moments and also one of my saddest. When I stared into their eyes and looked at their hopeless faces, I saw me. I felt their pain and anguish, because I was once in their shoes. I was poor and had come from a broken home. I was so broken, I thought I'd never be whole again.

As I closed my presentation, I offered the students words of encouragement (go figure). I told them, "Although your situations are unfortunate, continue to hold on, because it'll get better. The funny thing is, I was not only speaking to them, but to myself. Prior to God blessing me with that opportunity, I was slipping and losing my hope and grip on life. I wanted to let go, because I felt, "It hadn't happened, and it never would," whatever 'it' was. Later, things happened, but not in my timing, which seems to be the problem for most people. When I think of time, I think of it as being the last piece of the puzzle. In order for me to complete it, I have to wait on all the pieces to come together. That can be very hard and challenging, especially when you've waited for forever to finish, and now there's just one missing piece holding you up.

However, the one thing we feel is holding us up, is the very thing that's preparing us to move forward. Although we feel as though we're ready for the next move, sometimes we aren't. God causes us to wait, because He doesn't want us to destroy the blessing, all because we were unprepared. Suppose what would happen, had we gotten what we wanted without going through the process? I'm pretty sure we'd be overwhelmed and the things we were begging God to give us, we'd be begging Him to take back. You know why? When we ask God to bless us, He does it big. While our finite minds think so small in terms of our blessings, God's is completely infinite. There's no limit to what He can do. There aren't any obstacles in His way, and nothing is impossible for Him.

There were so many days that I thought I'd never get anything I prayed for. It seemed as if I kept sending up prayer requests, and they weren't going any farther than the ceiling. When I look back, I sometimes think what would've happened had I chosen to not hold on. One of the most profound quotes I've ever read, is from Germany Kent, which stated, "Don't give up when dark times come. The more storms you face in life, the stronger you'll be. Hold on. Your greater is coming." Regardless of what you are experiencing, the pain you feel, or how bleak things may look, be patient and wait on God. Pray and continue to hold on, because very soon, things will get better.

Adjust your view

Nothing is going right for me. No matter what I do, things still remain the same. I can't get ahead, because I'm always behind others. Everyone is rich, successful, and thriving, and I'm over here struggling to survive. It appears everyone is doing good, but me. I can't win for losing. Things never seem to go in my direction. For once, I wish I things would change for the better. Every time I turn around, if it's not one thing, it's another. Things have been going downhill for me, and I just can't see myself ever coming up again.

When I look back over all these statements I've made, I heard God say, "Deetra, the problem was never the view, it was always you." From your perspective, you saw, obstacles, defeat, and struggles. Yet from Mine, I saw expansion, resilience, and opportunity. While you looked at things pessimistically, I saw them optimistically, because I knew you could overcome anything that came your way, but first you had to believe you could.

There's no truer statement, than "seeing is believing." If you see yourself headed for disaster, you'll prepare for the impact, instead of preparing to bypass it. If you see hope, you'll be more prone to go towards it, than stay stuck in the darkness. Yet, if you see what God has for you, you'll be inclined to see things from His perspective. I know that can be extremely difficult to do, when you're only limited to what's in front of you. However, you've got to remember, nothing is always as it seems. The next time you feel nothing is working out for you, take a moment, and adjust your view. It's not your situation, but how you view it.

Hurting to heal

I love God! I know, shocker. Obviously, I was being facetious, but my relationship with God hasn't always been "that great." One of the biggest influences of that, has been the things I've gone through. For that reason alone, I used to be very angry and resentful towards God. I often questioned how can someone who says they love me, sit back, and watch me suffer? Especially, when it was within His power to change my situation. However, I continued to hurt, while resenting Him still. This went on for years, and things begin to look up for me, only to fall apart again. Like an elevator, I'd go up and down, up, and down, until I was down and couldn't seem to get back up. It seemed it was one terrible thing after the next, and the next thing I know, I was depressed and suicidal. Things had gotten so bad, I couldn't look for the positives, because I had become accustomed to negatives.

There's no way God could be with me, because it felt like He had left me. Not only was I hurting, but I was hurting alone. "God, you promised. You said you'd never leave me nor forsake me, yet I'm going through this by myself. Of all people in the world, why did you choose me? Why am I in pain?" He responded, "It's all a part of my plan. You might not understand it, but your hurt is going to help others heal." Everything I've gone through in my life, won't go to waste. I had to go through what I did, so I could help someone else get through their pain. I've come to the realization that things were never about me, but them. Did I like it? No, but it made me change my perspective of God and drew me closer than ever to Him. This journey hasn't been easy, but knowing my pain and suffering is only for a little while, makes it a little easier to continue on, instead of giving up. Remember, everything that involves you, isn't always about you!

Painful Profit

One night, I cried a river longer than the Jordan and Nile combined. Carrying burdens is a lot to deal with, especially when it seems as though you're carrying the load by yourself. Although God puts no more on us than we can bare, I can barely stand the little He does place on me. I say a little, because had it not being for His mercy, I would've experienced more than I have and gotten plenty of what I deserved. I've been caught in a years' long seasonal battle, and I've seriously questioned God whether or not there is indeed a way out, because being in is all I know.

I've done like many of you, cried, become upset, yell at or be angry with God. I'll admit, there were times I didn't pray or was reluctant to, because I already knew it wasn't going to "do any good." I've even stopped myself in the middle of crying and resided to the idea that it's not worth it. All of the sleepless nights and crying I'd experienced from hurting, was a complete waste, because when the tears stopped, my problems were still there. Either way, it made no difference to me, because I didn't see the difference I needed in my life.

I read in Psalms 56:8 that, "God keeps a track of my sorrows. He has collected all my tears in His bottle and recorded each one in His book (NLT)." For every tear that I've shed, God has taken notice. Not only was my sorrow not a waste, but as a result of what I've gone through, He's going to give me a profit for my pain. All of my trials, tribulations, and problems, God's got a record of. He sees and knows exactly what I'm facing, and not only is He facing it with me, He's going to help me make it through. Lately, I've felt like Peter and the Disciples in the boat, battling a great storm. Thinking it's the end, I call out to God, only for Him to command the wind not to move.

This season has been extremely hard on me, but having hope in the midst, is even harder. One day I was listening to an interview a singer did, and to paraphrase, she stated, "All I have left is my hope. Normally, it's the last thing to leave, but as long as I have it, they can't take it away from me, because once it's gone, I won't have anything left." I'm not sure of your situation or if you're at your wick's end, but if you are, there's one thing I want you to know, this too will end. You'll always have trouble, but eventually, they'll expire. No matter how many difficulties occur, keep praying and keep crying if you have too. God hears you, He sees you, and He's going to reward you for all of your pain.

The God of Suddenly

Have you ever gone through a period in your life, where you feel like nothing was going right? If it wasn't one thing, it was another? When it rained it poured? Nothing you did to get ahead worked, and no matter how many steps you took forward, you only appeared to be pushed back? You're still in the same place you were last year, and regardless of the numerous prayer requests, late night cries, and screams for God to help, you somehow managed to go unnoticed? Perhaps, you've given all you have to propel you to the next level of success, but even that's not enough, but I assure you it is.

The things you've long sought after, are going to come suddenly and unexpectedly. God has heard every cry and collected every tear in a bottle, so all that you've done, was not for nothing. It was used to build and prepare you for the position God has for you, but before you could take your rightful place up high, you had to first go to a place of complete trust and reliance upon God. Besides, if you didn't have Him, you'd think you did it on your own, and wouldn't have a need for Him. Truth of the matter, we all need Him. I don't care who you are or what you do, nothing that you have is a direct result of anything you did.

Just as God turned water into wine, fed 5,000 with ONLY 2 fish and 5 loaves of bread, He can turn your situation around suddenly! Don't think that just because it hasn't happened, it won't. You've got to give Him time to do it, and trust that He will! Sooner than later, you're going to have everything you've been praying for. It's already making its way to you. The question that remains is, "Are you ready for it?" Don't use the interim and waste it on doing nothing. Use this time wisely to prepare you for God's blessings. Trust me, you'll need too, especially if you knew the size of them.

A purpose for the flames

One Sunday at church, I had the wonderful pleasure of delivering the morning's message. I shared with my congregation the brave story of a woman named Deondra. Before I begin, I want to preface by saying, I don't know who you are, but you're not reading this book by happenstance. It's no coincidence that God led you to this book. He knew you needed it, as did I, therefore, He commissioned me to write it. I don't know of your whereabouts or position in life. I don't know if things are going great, good, or bad for you, but there's one thing that I do know. It is without a shadow of a doubt, that regardless of your circumstances, you can benefit and relate to Deondra's story.

Deondra is a 37-year-old woman who has had every curveball that life can pitch thrown at her. Miraculously, she's somehow managed to dodge them all. She's been extremely poor, depressed, contemplated suicide, and the list grows higher than Mount Everest. Disappointed in her circumstances, and even God, she felt things would never get better. However, as time passed and things remained the same, she began to lose faith and her hope was already gone. There were days, weeks, months, and years even, that she cried out to God to be saved, but there wasn't a rescue crew in sight. One day, in the midst of her pain, she yelled out to God, "If what I am experiencing is any indication of how my life is going to be, then I want out!"

Ultimately, her situation became too hot for her to handle, and because of her tiredness, she was ready to be consumed by the flames. However, God wouldn't allow it to happen. In Isaiah 43:2, He reminds us that, "When you walk through the fire of oppression, you will not be burned, and the flames will not consume you" (NLT). Instantly, I was reminded of the story of Shadrach, Meshach, and Abednego. As a result of their unwillingness to worship and acknowledge King Nebuchadnezzar as their God, he threw them into the fiery furnace. While his intent was for them to die, God intended to save them, and He did. He joined them in the fire, and upon noticing a fourth man inside, King Nebuchadnezzar called for Shadrach, Meshach, and Abednego to be released. Once out, they had no burn marks, their clothes nor hair was singed, neither did they reek of smoke.

Unlike the three men, DeOndra was so desperate for relief, she was willing to do anything to be saved, even if it meant giving up on God. Although she felt the heat, unbeknownst to her, God was already working to extinguish the flames. The flames were just too much for her to bear, but God promised He'd never put too much on us that we could bear. It didn't matter though, because Deondra still wanted her life to end. Sadly, she felt she had no purpose, so there wasn't any real purpose in living. As a result of her pain, she failed to realize that God had created her on purpose, with a purpose, and what she was experiencing was all a part of His purpose! God had a reason for her being, and He was not going to allow her to die, until she fulfilled His purpose.

When Deondra was going through all that pain and experienced one tragedy after the other, she didn't realize it then, what God was doing. He allowed her to go through all those trials, tribulations, and adversities, because He was preparing to use her for His glory. God gave her, "A crown of beauty, instead of ashes, the oil of joy, instead of mourning, and a garment of praise, instead of despair. The oaks of righteousness, the planting of the Lord for the display of His splendor" (Isaiah 61:3, NLT). Deondra later encountered many people from all walks of life, and they all shared one common thing, the fiery furnace. There were some people who were either still in the fire, on their way out of it or had made it out, and there were so many of them that stayed in. Since they were in the fire, they figured that things couldn't get any better, so there was no point in trying to escape.

Yet, it took Deondra sharing her story, for them to have hope and believe. Her thoughts and feelings were once theirs, so she knew it was another scare tactic the enemy was using to keep them bound. She remembered her days of desolation and despair, and how whenever she'd try to reframe her mind to focus on God's promises, the enemy would tell her things like, "If God cared so much about you, then why is He allowing you to go through all of this?" "If God is so mighty and powerful, and can do anything within the blink of an eye, why won't He change your situation?" He not only changed her life for the best, He used her to witness and share with others, all the wonderful things He had done for her. From that point forward, Deondra was a servant for the Lord, and hoped that others would see God in her and ultimately seek Him for themselves.

Are you in a situation that's unbearable and too hot to handle? Maybe, you're feeling the wrath of the fire and are wondering if you will ever make it out. Have you ever thought about ending your life, because you didn't see an end to your suffering? Perhaps you too feel as though you have no purpose in life. However, just as God had a purpose for Deondra, rest assured He has one for you too. I know things are pretty hot for you right now, but remember, there's a purpose for the flames. Continue to hang on, because your rescue is on the way. It may be taking God forever to come, but I promise, He hasn't forgotten about you. There's a lot of smoke now, but soon, He's going to make everything clear. By the way, for those of you wanting to know what happened to Deondra and how she's doing, I wanted to tell you all that, I'm doing just fine!

Looking for the rain

Whenever I'd see dark clouds form in the sky, it was an indication to me, that rain or a thunderstorm was very likely to come. In the event that it did, I would automatically do one of two things, grab an umbrella, or seek shelter. After I waited until the storm blew over, it amazed me to see things that were once filled with water, was suddenly dry. It was almost like it never rained. Suddenly, it reminded me of how Elijah, the Prophet, had prayed to God for 3.5 years for no rain, and it never came. As a result of the terrible famine and no harvest for food, Elijah went up to the mountain top and commissioned God to "make it rain."

At first, his request went unanswered. Then a second time. Then a third time. However, Elijah was persistent and sent his servant to go up to the mountain top a total of seven times, before he saw a dark cloud appear in the sky. Soon after, it rained. Elijah not only had guts, but he had faith as well. I've read that story countless of times, but now I see it differently. A lot of people equate dark clouds as a sign that something bad is about to happen, and in most cases, that's true. While some people wish the rain would never come, there are so many others looking for it.

Are you in a drought? Perhaps, you've gone to God countless of times praying for reprieve, yet you go "back down the mountain," carrying the same requests. You're almost to the point of giving up, but you continue to "make that climb," because you feel the next time is going to be it. I'm not sure about you, but I know I do! Although I'd like to be able to tell you when it's going to come, I can't. What I can tell you is, don't stop looking for the rain! Keep making your requests known, because eventually, God is going to send a downpour of His blessings. Just be patient and continue to wait on Him.

Faster than you can count

I'm not into Astrology, but I am pretty big on receiving signs. However, don't allow your obsession for signs or the need for confirmation, to cause you to constantly seek them, instead of God. For the past few years, at least the past three I know of, I have constantly seen the numbers 913. I see it everywhere I go, particularly, the clock. No matter when I look at it, 9:13 is what it reflects. Although one would associate the numbers 913 to be Angel Numbers, I simply don't ascribe to that ideology, nor anything tarot associated. Needless to say, my faith is in God, and not a deck of cards.

When God communicates with me specifically, it often comes through others, in my dreams, but mainly in scriptures. One of the many things I ask God for, is increase, whether that be in my finances or career. When I don't see an open door, I'm always reminded of God's word. Matthew 7:7 tells us to, "Ask and it will be given to you. Seek and ye shall find. Knock and the door would be opened unto you" (NLT). This doesn't just apply to me, but to everyone. After much prayer, fasting and seeking God, He not only revealed to me why I kept seeing the numbers 913, but He confirmed what I was praying (and expecting) for years.

He led me to Amos 9:13, which reads, "The time will come, says the Lord, when the grain and grapes will grow faster than they can be harvested (NLT)." He is Jehovah Jireh, "The One who provides," so anything that I need, He'll give it to me. In fact, His provisions will be in such an abundance, that the blessings will come faster than I can count them! I'm not sure who or what you put your trust or hopes in, but I can only hope that this gives you the confirmation that you need, and the courage to believe God to supply and take care of all your needs.

Buried (You've been planted) Pt. I

It's dark, cold, wet and you don't know where you are. You turn to your right, then left, but no matter which direction you go, you can't escape the blackness that surrounds you. That clammy, gritty substance you feel, is a result of the soil in which you've been submerged. Panic and anxiety creeps in, because you're at the bottom of the ground, and you don't see an opening in site. Unsure of your circumstances, how you got there or why you're there, you struggle for a way out, but as He would have it, you're unable to move. You've been planted! For how long, only God knows, so you might as well get used to your new home.

I know you don't like it, but in order for you to sprout, you've got to endure these conditions for a little while. I'm sure it's not what you want, but it's what you need. Although you think it's not necessary, it is. Besides, you're going to need pruning, before you can go to where He's taking you. Don't always look at the process as a being negative thing, but a learning experience. Once you emerge, you'll know why He kept you hidden for so long. Besides, anything of value takes time, and by no means are you a rushed job. Don't allow the length of the process, to keep you from growing.

What God has placed on the inside of you will grow, but you've got to endure the process and trust Him. Stop focusing on how hard things are and remind yourself of how there's nothing too hard for God. Besides, you can't prematurely rush what God is doing, because you won't be ready to receive the magnitude of what He has for you. It may take months or years of pruning, but the results will be worth the planting. You're in God's garden, so be patient, sit still and don't be in such a hurry to "grow" up!

Not yet (You've been planted) Pt. II

"Oh wow! You've got leaves! Beautiful, tiny, bright green leaves!" However, there are no petals attached. You're almost out, but things aren't quite rosy as they seem. You've made progress for sure, but something's still missing. You need more nourishment. I don't know if you realize it or not, but it's going to take more than water for you to come to life. Like many others, I'm pretty sure you thought you were just going to drop a few specks on your seed, come back in a few days and expect to see flowers. Sorry, but it doesn't quite work that way.

You've got to go through a nurturing process, and if you don't know anything about agriculture, understand this, water alone won't cause anything to grow! Talk to your seed (yourself), show yourself some love and speak your existence, into existence. It's dark, you're lonely and scared, probably frustrated too, but you've got to remain put! Just think, you started out as a tiny seed, now look how far you've come from the ground up! Your roots are strong, leaves have been established, but you've still got quite a ways to go. No doubt about it, you're going to bloom, but you're still not ready yet. Stay grounded for just a little while longer. I promise you, you're going to emerge soon!

I know God's process is taking a little longer than you anticipated, and you're beyond ready to come out. However, it's just not quite time, yet. You've still got a long way to go, before you finally evolve. Every day you're changing, and while you don't see it, God does. In fact, God sees a lot of things for you. Prosperity, peace, good health, and longevity can all be yours, but you've got to let God do His work! "But it's taking too long," you say. Since you seem to know, "Exactly how long is it supposed to take?" Did you think because you were buried, you were going to miraculously sprout up with no efforts at all?

Honestly, that's why so many of us stay submerged for so long, because no one wants to put in the work needed to reach their full potential. God gave you the blueprint, but it's up to you to build it. He didn't say He wouldn't help you, but He did say, "Faith without works is dead." Anything that's planted needs nourishment to grow, but you will never be able to successfully go through the proper stages of photosynthesis, because you're too busy shunning yourself from the very "Son" light you need. God is not punishing you for something that you've done, especially when He's already forgiven you for it. He's not harboring resentment or holding a grudge towards you, so stop assuming you aren't flourishing as you should, or as fast as you'd like, because you feel God is stunting your growth.

Besides, why would He bury you and expect you not to prosper? The question is, "Do you want to prosper?" In the beginning of the year 2020, I considered myself to be flourishing. I had a wonderful paying job, my personal life was thriving, and I was happier than I'd ever been before. I felt larger than life, until mine suddenly came crashing down. I didn't understand why God would allow me to grow so much in success, only for me to lose a couple of leaves. I felt as though I had been uprooted at the most inopportune time, because everything was rapidly moving, then suddenly the process stopped. Truthfully, it didn't stop. My growth did, once I became complacent. It's important to know that what you do in the process, determines if you continue to flourish or wither away. Have you ever thought that maybe you're stunting your growth?

The Emergence (You've been planted) Pt. III

Rise and shine, because now it's officially exposure time! You've been planted, watered, and nurtured, and now you're in full bloom! Consider yourself privileged, because you're in God's garden, planted amongst some of His finest creations. Everyone is looking at you and admiring your beauty, because they've never seen anything like you before. You're unique, radiant, beautiful to say the least, and you possess something no other flower has. Sure, we're all created in the likeness of His image, but your image is different. In fact, it's so different, the rest of the flowers (people) are asking why their seed isn't as powerful as yours. However, because no two flowers are alike, they won't ever look the same as you, let alone compete with your strength and ability to shine.

There was a reason you were buried, although you fought against it. There was a reason you were hidden, although you wanted to be out in the open. There was a reason you had to go through this lengthy, yet necessary process. There was a reason for everything God put you through, although you'll never understand it. He knew your worth, but I don't think you did. A lot of times we try to rush God, because we feel as though He's taking too long to get us to where we want to be, when essentially, it's not where He wants us to be. We'll adopt an "I'll take it from here attitude," and do what we feel is best. As a result of our stubbornness, we become stagnant and then wonder why we're stuck and can't "grow" any further. Sometimes, God places us in a position of uncomfortableness, which leaves us with no choice but to trust Him. Whatever you do, keep trusting and wait on Him! Now that you've endured the darkness, grew in the midst of what seemed to be an unbearable and uncomfortable situation, you have arisen and are well on your way out.

Just Ripe (You've been planted—The Conclusion)

Now is the time to reap the harvest! You've probably gone through one of the hardest processes of your life, but I'm sure it was all worth it. For what it's worth, you should be appreciative and beyond grateful, that God made you "take the stairs instead of riding the elevator." Sure, it took longer, but just think what would've happened had you taken the easy way out. More than likely, you probably wouldn't have made it this far, let alone at all. Because God is omniscient and we're not, He sees, hears, and knows about everything, including the people who plot and scheme to take you out. You've had many snares (people) set in place to create a diversion or worse, a disaster, because they know the power you possess. However, God knows the magnitude of the blessing He's buried on the inside of you, so He had to do what was necessary to protect His cause, and to see that it came to pass.

I know you didn't understand it, nor liked it, and probably questioned His reason for doing it. However, aren't you glad you went through what you did, to get to where you are? Who knows what would've happened, had He plucked you up before it was time to harvest. Let's just suppose that He had. What do you believe you would've looked like? Do you think you would've been as strong as you are now? Better yet, would you have been able to endure people trying to plant weeds around you, so they can take you out, well before you could even sprout? I can't explain to you why things happen as they do, and if I could, my only response would be timing. Now, do you understand why then was simply not your time? However, your time has now come! You are just ripe, and God is about to uproot you, so the entire world can see all that He has done for you!

Hard to believe

Sometimes I struggle with writing the messages God asks me to deliver to His people. The struggle is not that I don't know what to say, but actually believing what God gives me to say. As strange as it may seem, motivating, encouraging, and inspiring, is so easy and natural to me, but only when I do it for others. God speaks and instructs me what to write to uplift you, but then I'm left wondering, "What about me?" Majority, if not all, of what I write applies to and can help my circumstances, but it is extremely hard to believe that it will. That was hard for me to admit, because I was so fearful of being labeled a counterfeit, but more than anything, I want you to know, I'm just like you.

I go through long seasons of difficulty, moments of despair, hopelessness, and unbelief. I often question the validity of God's word, because I sometimes feel that what He says, doesn't align with my life. In fact, I'm still waiting to receive a lot of things He promised or said would happen for me, even though I wanted to give up a long time ago. If I'm being honest, I still want to give up now. However, no matter how hard I struggle to believe His word, I still hold on, because I know God is not a man that He should lie. More than anything, I want and need God's promises for my life. Although people have helped me in many ways, no one has come close to what God has done.

Often, I find myself running out of fuel, but I continue to have hope, even if it's just a little. God said we only need faith the size of a mustard seed, and at times, that's all I've got. I'm sure things will start to look up for me, and change my attitude for the better, but my problems are making it extremely hard to do. I'm not perfect, and I don't always know the right things to say, but what I can say is this, no matter how difficult things are, never stop believing, trusting, and having faith in God.

Waitlisted

My oldest sister loves luxury, designer, high-end, high-quality things. While she is not materialistic, she is a woman who gets what she wants, especially if she has the means to do so. For quite some time, I've known she's wanted a particular luxury purse. As a result of it being in high demand, she hasn't been able to get her hands on it. Nonetheless, she continued her search for it. After some time had passed, lo and behold, she was able to find the bag, but still unable to get it. I don't remember the exact reason why, whether it be the bag was out of stock or there were only a few of them, and too many people to accommodate for the shortage. Whatever the reason, she was waitlisted.

For most of my life, I like you, have been waiting on God for something. It doesn't matter how small or large I thought the request to be, it seemed as though it took forever for me to get it, and some I've still yet to receive. It can be extremely difficult to live life with a pleasant and optimistic attitude, when you're constantly being hit with blows from every angle. You feel so defeated and question if God is truly for you, especially when you have so many things coming up against you. It seems as though terrible things are constantly happening, one event right after the other, and you're left waiting, hoping, and praying, if God will ever join you in battle, because you've being going at it alone. However, you're not alone, because Deuteronomy 31:6 promises that "God will "never leave you, nor forsake you" (NLT).

Do you feel like you've been waitlisted by God? For years, you've prayed to Him for financial increase, a husband, wife, children, healing, a house, a car, and a better job, only to find yourself still without it. When you look around, you see everyone getting what you've desired, and you're left wondering, "God, when will it be my turn?" You start to feel as though He's forgotten about you, and nothing you've prayed for will ever come to pass. Besides, you've been praying for it for so long and you still don't have it, so you think, maybe it wasn't intended for you. However, just because you don't see it, doesn't mean it isn't there. It is and always has. It's just making its way to you. Until then, wait with excitement, because you know, after a while, God will remove you from the waitlist.

Don't leave the waiting room

Are you frustrated, tired, and hopeless? Do you often find yourself crying, or angrily screaming at God to fix your problems? Do you feel like giving up and walking away from your situation? Are you doubtful that things will ever get better for you? Do you feel like you're fighting a never-ending battle? Are you sick, depressed, anxious, or feel defeated? Do you feel forgotten? Do you feel like you've always been the one to help others, but now you have no one there for you? Are you jealous when you see people undeservingly get the things you've been praying for years for? Are you beginning to shy away from praying, because you don't see any of them being answered? As if all of that's not enough, have you grown beyond tired from waiting on God?

If you've answered yes to either of those questions, God told me to tell you, He knows. Not only does He know what you're going through, but He's going to see you through it. I'm sure if you polled 100 people what's the one thing you don't like doing, I guarantee you, more than 25% will say, waiting. I'm not sure if we can attribute that to societal pressures, or our own impatience. Whichever the case, waiting is not something most would happily want to do, especially when they are going through seasons of difficulty. James 1:2-3 tells us, "Consider it pure joy, my brothers and sisters, whenever you face trials of many kinds, because you know that the testing of your faith produces perseverance (NLT)." Let's be honest, who's worried about persevering, when they're struggling? I for one, didn't, because I was too focused on what I was going through, as opposed to making it through.

I mentioned this earlier in this book, and for those of you like me, who are tired of hearing, "be patient and wait on God," I think this deserves another mention. Over a year ago, a position that I was in was eliminated. That was the best job I've ever had, and I not only loved what I did, I loved going to work. In fact, I got up super early every day rushing to get there. My eyebrows were always raised with regards to management, and I kept an uneasy feeling when I was around them. Behind the façade, I could see all the sugar, honey, iced tea, they were filled with. Even still, I had a job to do, and I did it very well. Needless to say, people felt threatened by me, and I presume they did what they thought they needed to do, by ridding me of my position.

I'm not sure if the motive was jealousy or not, but what I do know is, when God told me not to fight it and just move, I simply followed His lead. Some months after, I felt so free, relieved, and happy. Although I missed what I did, and who I did it for, I didn't miss being in an environment that threatened my peace of mind. With that now behind me, I was ready to move full steam ahead, with the plans God had for me. After what I went through in my life, and all the crap I dealt with, I just knew God was about to expeditiously catapult me to the top. Prior to my exit, I remember saying, "God I know you are about to quickly open many doors of opportunity for me, but if you need me to crawl again before I can walk through them, I will." Regrettably, I questioned why on earth would I say that! Not only did I crawl, I struggled too. With a blink of an eye, my happiness turned to remorse and anger, because there I was following God, and He all of a suddenly just left me. I felt a little betrayed by Him, honestly, because I thought I was doing what He wanted me to do, yet I was going down a slippery slope fast.

Like the domino effect, when one thing fell, all the others fell right behind. My bills were past due, my truck was almost repossessed, I was almost evicted from my apartment, I had no savings in the bank, nor did I have money to buy food. I grew up on government assistance (i.e. food stamps) and I promised once those days were over, I was never going back. Yet there I was applying for them. I thought so many times, "There is no way this is my life. God why did you allow this to happen?" He blessed me with a luxury apartment, luxury truck, and so many other nice things, but all of a sudden, He was now being mean to me. I felt punished, and I kept wondering, what had I done to warrant such a harsh life.

My mental health suffered tremendously, I was depressed, sad, and angry all the time. Every time my sister purchased a new luxury bag, I cringed, and quietly said, "There goes my rent, car payment, and car insurance. In no way am I stating that my sister sat by and watched as I slid further into a black hole, while she shopped until she dropped, because she did help me on a few occasions. Honestly, had it not been for my mom's love and support, and my nieces and nephew, I probably would've killed myself a long time ago. They are the reasons I was able to muster up the strength to keep going. My church family has stepped up and in on so many occasions, I often wonder how I'm going to repay them back. I feel so privileged, blessed, and lucky even, to have such a large church family in my corner, who not only cares about me, but constantly prays and provides for me, and I thank God for using them to do it. I'm eternally grateful for everyone who has helped me in my time of need, because their generosity and God's strength is what gave me the nudge I needed to continue on, despite what my situation looked like.

Even though God was using them to pull me up, my situation kept weighing me down. I felt so defenseless and helpless, and not like myself. Truthfully, I didn't know who in the hell I was. My self-esteem dropped to an all-time low, my skin broke out, and my hair had fallen out so bad, it left me with bald spots all over my head. My weight was up (again), and for the first time ever in my life, my blood pressure was high. At that point, I felt like that 14-year-old suicidal little girl I used to be, and I desperately wanted my life to end. There were days I'd wake up crying, mad, and angry at God, for allowing me to see another day. I was an emotional wreck and wondered if I'd ever recover again.

I know people always say that God is with you in the midst of the storm, but I felt very alone. I thought, if you calmed the storm for Peter, God why won't you do it for me? Truthfully, my thoughts were all of the place. One minute I'd be up and the next, I'd be down again. I kept trying to remind myself that trouble don't last always, but my on-going situation proved otherwise. Later down the line, I ended up being hired as a temporary employee, with no benefits (health or life) and little pay. Suddenly, I began to wonder if I'd made the right decision by declining that other position and following God. However, regardless of what my circumstances were, I knew God was taking me somewhere.

By far, that was the most stressful, depressing and emotionally draining job I'd ever had. I was sick pretty much most of the time, but like the faithful, hardworking, over achieving person I am, I endured. My days were long and exhausting, and I'd cry in my truck before I went in, because I knew that job was not what I wanted, but it was helping to pay my bills. To make matters worse, majority of the people I encountered there were rude, standoffish, expressed no desire to help, and thought they were better than me, because they were gainfully employed, and I was "just a temp," a word they often used to describe me.

Although their attitudes towards me was extremely poor, I never stopped doing my job. I was committed to excellency and being of service to our customers. Despite what I was dealing with professionally and personally, it never affected my work performance. In fact, I was constantly exceeding my goals, and often received many compliments and high praise, from our customers and employees alike. Granted there were quite a few bad apples there, thankfully they didn't spoil the entire bunch. I was very fortunate, or blessed I should say, to have met some really sweet, kind, and caring people. One lady in particular, worked on the same floor as me, and as my sister would say, "she was sweetness overload." If you ever desired an outgoing, full of life, cheerful, thoughtful, considerate friend, or someone exuding extreme positivity, she was the one! I could tell she woke up on 10 everyday, ready to conquer the world, and spread love, peace, and joy.

If I'm being honest, no matter how angry or upset I was with God for not immediately changing my situation, I realized He was working to change me. Although I still struggle, I came to terms with that job being another stepping stone God was using, to ultimately take me to where He wanted me to be. I'm not going to pretend and say that I liked being "the chosen one" God used to go through trials, tribulations, and times of difficulty, to help other people. I won't even tell you I waited with patience and joy, as I made my way through it all. What I will tell you is, no matter how sick, down, depressed, upset, hurt, or angry I was, I knew God was working everything out for my good. Had it not been for His mercy, grace, favor, protection, and strength, I know for a fact, I would've lost my mind! Truthfully, there were times I thought I had.

Although I'm not yet over the hump, I know pretty soon I will be. I also know that even though I don't have financial stability, my mansion, successful business, spouse, twins, or best-selling books, doesn't mean that I won't ever. It's all making its way to me, and as I await its arrival, I'll continue to remain seated, patient, and won't leave the waiting room. The enemy will tempt you, enlarge your problems bigger than what they are, and repeatedly tell you God is not doing anything about your situation. The enemy is the father of lies, so whatever you do, don't believe him. You've probably been in the waiting room for years, and God still hasn't called your name yet. Remember, it's coming, and there's nothing anyone can do to stop what God has for you, not the devil, and not even you. It's hard being courageous and strong, when defeat seems within arm's reach. Nonetheless, reach for your Bible, study, and apply God's word to your life, and wait until you're called. The question is, will you be ready?

I'm proud of my journey, because it is shaping me into the woman God has purposed me to be. I may have had many low points in my life, opposed to highs, but I know very soon, I'll be able to look down, extend a hand, and help others to get to where I will be. That space in between the dream and the promise, requires patience and constant prayer. You cannot grow weary or allow fear, anxiety, and the unknown, to cause you to miss the promise. You can't afford to sit idle either, but instead prepare yourself to be in position to receive God's promise, because He won't give you something you aren't ready for. If that be the case, you'd end up mismanaging your blessings, and become so overwhelmed, that you end up asking God to take back what He gave. The interim can be a lonely place, but it's also the place that promotes change. If you want God to change your circumstances, change your attitude towards waiting.

Surviving the wait

I used to think God was punishing me, because whenever I'd pray to Him, He didn't give me an answer, at least not the one I wanted anyway. I would get so angry and upset with Him, because He said that "He would never leave me nor forsake me," yet I've always felt so alone. I can remember very vividly being in church amongst believers, wondering what they'd think of me, if they knew I really didn't believe God or much of anything He said. I know that He is real and does exist, but I couldn't help but question, "How can God say He loves me and is able to sit back and watch me suffer, and do nothing at all?" I didn't find anything loving about someone who has power to change my situation, but instead allowed me to remain in it. I kept thinking, "Surely, God is not all people made Him out to be," because when you love someone, you do whatever you can to help them, not harm them.

Although I was not physically in danger, (if you count all the times I've contemplated suicide, then I guess you can say that I was), mentally I was in an all-out guerilla warfare. My mind was so fried, nearly to the point of ruins, because I constantly thought, "Why is God doing this to me? Haven't I suffered enough?" Must I remind you, the peak of my trials, tribulations and suicide thoughts occurred when I was a teenager. Can you explain to me what a teenager could have done, that warranted such harsh treatment? Neither did I, so I just hid my pain and turned my back to God, because I felt He had done the same to me. This continued for years, and my attitude and feelings only worsened, much like my situation. I can remember going to bed pouting, fussing, and laying blame to God, because I faulted Him for my sufferings. I seriously thought I was doing Him damage by not praying, but I was only causing myself pure harm.

The gall of me to even think I could hurt God, but I only did it because I was hurting. I was depressed, discouraged, and disappointed, because I thought my life would never get any better. I can honestly say that God has used a lot of people to bless me, but best of all, to pray for me. I can't begin to tell you how that not only changed my life, but it changed my attitude and feelings towards God. I felt so foolish, ashamed, and embarrassed even, because the one person I thought had turned their back on me, was beside me all along. He never went anywhere, I did. In fact, there were a lot of things that I did differently from that point forward. I begin to worship and praise God more. I began to "trust in Him with all my heart and lean not on my own understanding." I prayed constantly, and I made it my mission to not only tell everyone I encountered about God, but I boasted about all the wonderful things He had done for me.

I didn't understand it before, but in hindsight, I realize what all the "hype" or praise I should say, was about. When I would see the ladies running and shouting in church, I thought it was a façade or a show to see who could "out praise" the other. However, all they were showing was thanksgiving to God, and I should have too. When I'd hear them yell out, "Thank you Lord," I quietly mumbled the same, because of what He had not only done for them, but for me as well. When I saw people crying, praising, and singing, I saw the miracles, healings, and breakthroughs, but best of all, I saw what God was doing through me. My misfortunes had nothing to do with me. It was all about Him. God wanted the glory, and He just used me to get it. I never wanted the assignment, but the Teacher doesn't give you what you want, He gives you what you need. I needed that lesson, but more than anything, I needed God to take me through the fire, so my testimony would cause others to burn with worship, adoration, and praise for Him.

When I first started writing this book, I debated whether or not I should. One, I didn't want to sound "too preachy," and two, I didn't want to misrepresent God. I'm sure everyone has their own personal beliefs, experiences, and criticisms of this book, but I didn't write it for judgement. I wrote it to serve as a witness to God and hopes of others seeking Him for themselves. The premise of this book is learning to be patient, and to show you how things would work out for our good, if we wait on God. When we jump the gun and get ahead of ourselves, and God, we tend to make mistakes. Afterwards, we're left wondering what happened, while soliciting God to clean up our mess once again. I used to think I was such a "big girl" and could do things all by myself, but when life became too hard, I quickly realized how desperately I needed God's help. Not only did I need His help, I wanted it!

Speaking of want, isn't that how we end up in most of the predicaments we get in, because of doing what *we want* to do? We foolishly do as we see fit, and then we lose control, we quickly yell, "Jesus take the wheel." When I took charge and drove, I experienced so many incidents and dead ends, that I didn't mind becoming a passenger. Besides, I had gotten so tired of thinking "I had arrived at my destination," only for God to tell me to make a U-turn. Most of the time, I couldn't navigate my way through everyday tasks, so I don't know why I supposed I could find my way in life, at least not without the help of my GPS (God's Protecting Spirit). Following Him has been the best and most rewarding thing that's ever happened to me! Over the years, I've learned a lot of valuable things, but being still and waiting on God to move, is most important. This has been an incredibly long journey, and I didn't think I'd ever make it, but because of God's amazing grace, I am surviving the wait!

About the Author

Deetra La'Rue is the 2020 recipient of the West Montgomery District Coretta Scott King Award, and author of 5 novels including, *Glitter but no gold: How I turned my wounds into wisdom, and Words are weapons too! Understanding the power of words.* She lives in historical Montgomery, Alabama, which is the birthplace to the Montgomery Bus Boycott Movement, the Civil Rights Movement, and the Selma to Montgomery March. Although she's no Whitney Houston, she thoroughly loves singing, but knows that writing is clearly her gift. When not writing, she enjoys volunteering, speaking to disadvantaged and underrepresented students, fashion, red lipstick and creating inspirational content for her blog, *Notes by La'Rue*. Please visit Deetra at notesbylarue.com to get your daily "notes" of inspiration!

www.ingramcontent.com/pod-product-compliance
Lightning Source LLC
Chambersburg PA
CBHW081018040426
42444CB00014B/3264